T0231209

Internet Applications
of Type II Uses of Technology
in Education

Internet Applications of Type II Uses of Technology in Education has been co-published simultaneously as *Computers in the Schools*, Volume 22, Numbers 1/2 2005.

Monographic Separates from *Computers in the Schools*

For additional information on these and other Haworth Press titles, including descriptions, tables of contents, reviews, and prices, use the QuickSearch catalog at http://www.HaworthPress.com.

Internet Applications of Type II Uses of Technology in Education, edited by Cleborne D. Maddux, PhD, and D. LaMont Johnson, PhD (Vol. 22, No. 1/2, 2005). *An overview of effective Type II teaching applications that use technology to develop new and better strategies for learning.*

Web-Based Learning in K-12 Classrooms: Opportunities and Challenges, edited by Jay Blanchard, PhD, and James Marshall, PhD (Vol. 21, No. 3/4, 2004). *Examines the possibilities of today's online learning applications across the K-12 curriculum.*

Integrating Information Technology into the Teacher Education Curriculum: Process and Products of Change, edited by Nancy Wentworth, PhD, Rodney Earle, PhD, and Michael L. Connell, PhD (Vol. 21, No. 1/2, 2004). *A powerful reference for teacher education departments striving to integrate new technologies into their curriculum and motivate their faculty to utilize them.*

Distance Education: What Works Well, edited by Michael Corry, PhD, and Chih-Hsuing Tu, PhD (Vol. 20, No. 3, 2003). *"A must read. . . . Provides a highly readable, practical, yet critical perspective into the design, delivery, and implementation of distance learning. . . . Examines issues faced by distance educators, offers valuable tactics culled from experience, and outlines strategies that have been key success factors for a wide variety of distance learning initiatives." (Veena Mahesh, PhD, Distance and Blended Learning Program Manager, Technology Manufacturing Group Training, Intel Corporation)*

Technology in Education: A Twenty-Year Retrospective, edited by D. LaMont Johnson, PhD, and Cleborne D. Maddux, PhD (Vol. 20, No. 1/2, 2003). *"Interesting, informative, relevant. . . . Having so many experts between the covers of one book was a treat. . . . I enjoyed reading this book!" (Susan W. Brown, PhD, Science/Math Methods Professor and Professional Curriculum Coordinator, New Mexico State University)*

Distance Education: Issues and Concerns, edited by Cleborne D. Maddux, PhD, Jacque Ewing-Taylor, MS, and D. LaMont Johnson, PhD (Vol. 19, No. 3/4, 2002). *Provides practical, research-based advice on distance education course design.*

Evaluation and Assessment in Educational Information Technology, edited by Leping Liu, PhD, D. LaMont Johnson, PhD, Cleborne D. Maddux, PhD, and Norma J. Henderson, MS (Vol. 18, No. 2/3 and 4, 2001). *Explores current trends, issues, strategies, and methods of evaluation and assessment in educational information technology.*

The Web in Higher Education: Assessing the Impact and Fulfilling the Potential, edited by Cleborne D. Maddux, PhD, and D. LaMont Johnson, PhD (Vol. 17, No. 3/4 and Vol. 18, No. 1, 2001). *"I enthusiastically recommend this book to anyone new to Web-based program development. I am certain that my project has moved along more rapidly because of what I learned from this text. The chapter on designing online education courses helped to organize my programmatic thinking. Another chapter did an outstanding job of debunking the myths regarding Web learning." (Carol Swift, PhD, Associate Professor and Chair of the Department of Human Development and Child Studies, Oakland University, Rochester, Michigan)*

Using Information Technology in Mathematics Education, edited by D. James Tooke, PhD, and Norma Henderson, MS (Vol. 17, No. 1/2, 2001). *"Provides thought-provoking material on several aspects and levels of mathematics education. The ideas presented will provide food for thought for the reader, suggest new methods for the classroom, and give new ideas for further research." (Charles E. Lamb, EdD, Professor, Mathematics Education, Department of Teaching, Learning, and Culture, College of Education, Texas A&M University, College Station)*

Integration of Technology into the Classroom: Case Studies, edited by D. LaMont Johnson, PhD, Cleborne D. Maddux, PhD, and Leping Liu, PhD (Vol. 16, No. 2/3/4, 2000). *Use these fascinating case studies to understand why bringing information technology into your classroom can make you a more effective teacher, and how to go about it!*

Information Technology in Educational Research and Statistics, edited by Leping Liu, PhD, D. LaMont Johnson, PhD, and Cleborne D. Maddux, PhD (Vol. 15, No. 3/4, and Vol. 16, No. 1, 1999). *This important book focuses on creating new ideas for using educational technologies such as the Internet, the World Wide Web and various software packages to further research and statistics. You will explore on-going debates relating to the theory of research, research methodology, and successful practices.* Information Technology in Educational Research and Statistics *also covers the debate on what statistical procedures are appropriate for what kinds of research designs.*

Educational Computing in the Schools: Technology, Communication, and Literacy, edited by Jay Blanchard, PhD (Vol. 15, No. 1, 1999). *Examines critical issues of technology, teaching, and learning in three areas: access, communication, and literacy. You will discover new ideas and practices for gaining access to and using technology in education from preschool through higher education.*

Logo: A Retrospective, edited by Cleborne D. Maddux, PhD, and D. LaMont Johnson, PhD (Vol. 14, No. 1/2, 1997). *"This book–honest and optimistic–is a must for those interested in any aspect of Logo: its history, the effects of its use, or its general role in education." (Dorothy M. Fitch, Logo consultant, writer, and editor, Derry, New Hampshire)*

Using Technology in the Classroom, edited by D. LaMont Johnson, PhD, Cleborne D. Maddux, PhD, and Leping Liu, MS (Vol. 13, No. 1/2, 1997). *"A guide to teaching with technology that emphasizes the advantages of transiting from teacher-directed learning to learner-centered learning–a shift that can draw in even 'at-risk' kids." (Book News, Inc.)*

Multimedia and Megachange: New Roles for Educational Computing, edited by W. Michael Reed, PhD, John K. Burton, PhD, and Min Liu, EdD (Vol. 10, No. 1/2/3/4, 1995). *"Describes and analyzes issues and trends that might set research and development agenda for educators in the near future." (Sci Tech Book News)*

Language Minority Students and Computers, edited by Christian J. Faltis, PhD, and Robert A. DeVillar, PhD (Vol. 7, No. 1/2, 1990). *"Professionals in the field of language minority education, including ESL and bilingual education, will cheer this collection of articles written by highly respected, research-writers, along with computer technologists, and classroom practitioners." (Journal of Computing in Teacher Education)*

Logo: Methods and Curriculum for Teachers, by Cleborne D. Maddux, PhD, and D. LaMont Johnson, PhD (Supp #3, 1989). *"An excellent introduction to this programming language for children." (Rena B. Lewis, Professor, College of Education, San Diego State University)*

Assessing the Impact of Computer-Based Instruction: A Review of Recent Research, by M. D. Roblyer, PhD, W. H. Castine, PhD, and F. J. King, PhD (Vol. 5, No. 3/4, 1988). *"A comprehensive and up-to-date review of the effects of computer applications on student achievement and attitudes." (Measurements & Control)*

Educational Computing and Problem Solving, edited by W. Michael Reed, PhD, and John K. Burton, PhD (Vol. 4, No. 3/4, 1988). *Here is everything that educators will need to know to use computers to improve higher level skills such as problem solving and critical thinking.*

The Computer in Reading and Language Arts, edited by Jay S. Blanchard, PhD, and George E. Mason, PhD (Vol. 4, No. 1, 1987). *"All of the [chapters] in this collection are useful, guiding the teacher unfamiliar with classroom computer use through a large number of available software options and classroom strategies." (Educational Technology)*

Computers in the Special Education Classroom, edited by D. LaMont Johnson, PhD, Cleborne D. Maddux, PhD, and Ann Candler, PhD (Vol. 3, No. 3/4, 1987). *"A good introduction to the use of computers in special education. . . . Excellent for those who need to become familiar with computer usage with special population students because they are contemplating it or because they have actually just begun to do it." (Science Books and Films)*

You Can Do It/Together, by Kathleen A. Smith, PhD, Cleborne D. Maddux, PhD, and D. LaMont Johnson, PhD (Supp #2, 1986). *A self-instructional textbook with an emphasis on the partnership system of learning that introduces the reader to four critical areas of computer technology.*

Computers and Teacher Training: A Practical Guide, by Dennis M. Adams, PhD (Supp #1, 1986). *"A very fine . . . introduction to computer applications in education." (International Reading Association)*

The Computer as an Educational Tool, edited by Henry F. Olds, Jr. (Vol. 3, No. 1, 1986). *"The category of tool uses for computers holds the greatest promise for learning, and this . . . book, compiled from the experiences of a good mix of practitioners and theorists, explains how and why." (Jack Turner, Technology Coordinator, Eugene School District 4-J, Oregon)*

Logo in the Schools, edited by Cleborne D. Maddux, PhD (Vol. 2, No. 2/3, 1985). *"An excellent blend of enthusiasm for the language of Logo mixed with empirical analysis of the language's effectiveness as a means of promoting educational goals. A much-needed book!" (Rena Lewis, PhD, Professor, College of Education, San Diego State University)*

Humanistic Perspectives on Computers in the Schools, edited by Steven Harlow, PhD (Vol. 1, No. 4, 1985). *"A wide spectrum of information." (Infochange)*

Internet Applications
of Type II Uses of Technology
in Education

Cleborne D. Maddux
D. LaMont Johnson
Editors

Internet Applications of Type II Uses of Technology in Education has been co-published simultaneously as *Computers in the Schools*, Volume 22, Numbers 1/2 2005.

Routledge
Taylor & Francis Group

NEW YORK AND LONDON

First Published by

The Haworth Integrative Healing Press is an imprint of The Haworth Press, Inc., 10 Alice Street, Binghamton, NY 13904-1580 USA.

Transferred to Digital Printing 2011 by Routladge
711 Third Avenue, New York, NY 10017
2 Park Square, Milton Park, Abingdon, Oxon, OX14 4RN

Internet Applications of Type II Uses of Technology in Education has been co-published simultaneously as *Computers in the Schools*, Volume 22, Numbers 1/2 2005.

© 2005 by The Haworth Press, Inc. All rights reserved. No part of this work may be reproduced or utilized in any form or by any means, electronic or mechanical, including photocopying, microfilm and recording, or by any information storage and retrieval system, without permission in writing from the publisher.

The development, preparation, and publication of this work has been undertaken with great care. However, the publisher, employees, editors, and agents of The Haworth Press and all imprints of The Haworth Press, Inc., including The Haworth Medical Press® and Pharmaceutical Products Press®, are not responsible for any errors contained herein or for consequences that may ensue from use of materials or information contained in this work. Opinions expressed by the author(s) are not necessarily those of The Haworth Press, Inc. With regard to case studies, identities and circumstances of individuals discussed herein have been changed to protect confidentiality. Any resemblance to actual persons, living or dead, is entirely coincidental.

Cover design by Wendy Arakawa

Library of Congress Cataloging-in-Publication Data

Maddux, Cleborne D., 1942-
    Internet applications of Type II uses of technology in education / Cleborne D. Maddux, D. LaMont Johnson, editors.
        p. cm.
    "Co-published simultaneously as Computers in the Schools, Volume 22, Numbers 1/2 2005."
    Includes bibliographical references and index.
    ISBN-13: 978-0-7890-2494-7 (hard cover : alk. paper)
    ISBN-10: 0-7890-2494-2 (hard cover : alk. paper)
    ISBN-13: 978-0-7890-2495-4 (soft cover : alk. paper)
    ISBN-10: 0-7890-2495-0 (soft cover : alk. paper)
    1. Educational technology–United States. 2. Internet in education–United States. 3. Computer-assisted instruction–United States. I. Johnson, D. LaMont (Dee LaMont), 1939- II. Computers in the schools. III. Title.

LB1028.3.M334 2005
371.33′4–dc22
                                                                                2005008528

Internet Applications
of Type II Uses of Technology
in Education

Contents

ABOUT THE EDITORS

Cleborne D. Maddux, PhD, is Foundation Professor in the Department of Counseling and Educational Psychology at the University of Nevada, Reno, where he teaches courses on statistics and on integrating technology into education. He has co-authored 10 books with D. LaMont Johnson, including *Distance Education: Issues and Concerns* and the textbook *Educational Computing: Learning with Tomorrow's Technologies*, now in its third edition.

D. LaMont Johnson, PhD, Professor of Educational Technology in the College of Education at the University of Nevada, Reno (UNR), is a leading specialist in the area of educational computing and related technologies. He is the founding editor of *Computers in the Schools* and is Program Coordinator of the Information Technology in Education program at UNR. He has co-authored 10 books, including *Distance Education: Issues and Concerns* and the textbook *Educational Computing: Learning with Tomorrow's Technologies*, now in its third edition. A popular speaker and conference presenter, Dr. Johnson is active in several professional organizations concerned with advancing the use and understanding of educational technology.

INTRODUCTION

Cleborne D. Maddux
D. LaMont Johnson

Type II Applications
of Technology in Education:
New and Better Ways of Teaching
and Learning

This special double issue of *Computers in the Schools* is dedicated to articles exploring the use of Type II applications of technology in education. The Type I/Type II concept has its origin in countless early conversations involving the two of us, and to a 1984 article published in the introductory issue of this journal entitled *Educational Microcomputing: The Need for Research* (Maddux, 1984).

CLEBORNE D. MADDUX is Associate Editor for Research, *Computers in the Schools*, and Foundation Professor, Department of Counseling and Educational Psychology, University of Nevada, Reno, Reno, NV 89557 (E-mail: maddux@unr.edu). D. LAMONT JOHNSON is Professor, Department of Counseling and Educational Psychology, College of Education, University of Nevada, Reno, Reno, NV 89557 (E-mail: ljohnson@unr.edu).

[Haworth co-indexing entry note]: "Type II Applications of Technology in Education: New and Better Ways of Teaching and Learning." Maddux, Cleborne D., and D. LaMont Johnson. Co-published simultaneously in *Computers in the Schools* (The Haworth Press, Inc.) Vol. 22, No. 1/2, 2005, pp. 1-5; and: *Internet Applications of Type II Uses of Technology in Education* (ed: Cleborne D. Maddux, and D. LaMont Johnson) The Haworth Press, Inc., 2005, pp. 1-5. Single or multiple copies of this article are available for a fee from The Haworth Document Delivery Service [1-800-HAWORTH, 9:00 a.m. - 5:00 p.m. (EST). E-mail address: docdelivery@haworthpress.com].

Available online at http://www.haworthpress.com/web/CITS
© 2005 by The Haworth Press, Inc. All rights reserved.
Digital Object Identifier: 10.1300/J025v22n01_01

At that time, the idea of categorizing technology applications in education as Type I or Type II had just occurred to us, and it evolved from our concern that computers in schools were being poorly used. Drill-and-practice programs were the most common educational software found in schools at the time, and we feared that the gap between the lofty, overblown claims of technology advocates and the boring and mundane uses to which computers were often being applied had set the stage for a major backlash against bringing computers into schools.

Neither of us can remember when we first began talking about Type I and Type II applications, nor when we first began referring to them by those specific terms. However, we both remember two experiences that were so diametrically different that they undoubtedly influenced us to begin thinking in terms of a dichotomy.

In the first instance, we were both professors at Texas Tech University, and we were invited to visit a local school to view a new computer lab and to observe the teacher in charge working with a group of students. We arrived to find the class in session, with each student seated at a then-state-of-the-art computer. The teacher was seated at a desk at the front of the room grading papers while a tape recorder droned on in a monotone rhythm: *"Now type A" (pause) "Now type S" (pause) "Now type D" (pause)*, and so on, for the entire period. We went away discouraged, thinking that such uses were a kind of *educational reverse alchemy*, in which gold was being turned into lead.

About this same time, we had an experience at the other end of the spectrum. We were invited to visit Texas Instruments' educational software development department, where the Logo computer language was being prepared for use with the TI99/4A computer, at that time a very impressive, 16-bit computer with excellent graphics. The development team was excited and exciting, and the TI99/4A implementation of Logo was the best available, and far ahead of its time. We left TI that day with our enthusiasm for technology renewed, and our belief in its potential to improve teaching and learning restored.

Those incidents may have been the impetus for the idea of Type I/Type II applications. In the first CIS article, the idea was embryonic, and Type I uses were defined simply as those applications of technology in education that "simply help us to continue teaching the same things in pretty much the same ways we have always taught them," while Type II applications "are those uses which constitute new and better ways of teaching" (Maddux, 1984, p. 38).

We continued to refer to Type I and Type II uses in our speaking engagements and our writing over the next couple of years, and we enlarged upon the idea in another, later article in *Computers in the Schools* (Maddux, 1986). The two of us had been thinking about the concept and discussing it at length. In that article, it was emphasized that Type I and Type II applications were not a simple dichotomy that represented bad and good practices. Rather, we concluded that good examples of Type I applications were to be encouraged and should be used in schools. We agreed, however, that Type I applications were not sufficiently powerful by themselves to justify the investment in time, money, and enthusiasm required to bring them into schools. Instead, we thought, it would take excellent examples of both Type I and Type II applications if computers in schools were to succeed. We did, however, conclude that Type II applications were the more promising of the two types. Unfortunately, they were then, and remain today the more scarce of the two types, and the more difficult to develop and use in an educationally advantageous way.

We continued to think in terms of Type I and Type II applications, and in 1986 and 1987, two articles dealing with the concept were published, one in *Educational Technology* (Maddux & Cummings, 1986) and one in *The Computing Teacher* (Maddux & Cummings, 1987). *The Computing Teacher* featured the two types on the cover of the journal that month, with each type depicted as a door that represented a choice. In both articles, we explained the categories more fully, as illustrated by the following quotation from the 1987 article:

> We have found it useful to categorize computer applications as either Type I or Type II. Type I usage predominates and uses computing to make traditional teaching methods easier or more efficient. User involvement is relatively passive, and what happens on the screen is largely predetermined by the programmer. Rote skills are emphasized, and the computer is too frequently employed as an electronic flashcard machine. Type II usage, on the other hand, employs computers to make available new and better ways of teaching children. The user is the most important actor in the interaction and is the primary controller of what happens on the screen. Problem solving and other thinking skills are emphasized, and the computer is employed as a tool to aid cognitive processes. Examples of Type II usage are programming, simulations, and word processing. (p. 16)

The concept seemed useful to some people, and when the two of us and Jerry Willis collaborated on our educational computing textbook

(Maddux, Johnson, & Willis, 1992, 1997, 2001), we organized all three editions of the text around the concept of Type I/Type II applications. We continued to use this categorization scheme in our speaking engagements and in our writing, and others began using the Type I and Type II terminology in their professional work.

Nevertheless, we were unsure whether or not there was enough interest to support LaMont Johnson's idea for the two of us to edit a special issue of this journal on Type II applications. We were, however, amazed at the response to our call for papers. Because the response was so overwhelming, we first decided to do one double special issue, then expanded the plan to two double special issues, and finally settled on three double special issues of *Computers in the Schools* dedicated to articles on Type II applications. Even so, we were forced to reject many deserving articles because there was simply no room to include all the excellent manuscripts we received. For that we apologize, and we wish to express our sincere gratitude to the many individuals who took the time and devoted the effort needed to produce a manuscript for our consideration.

Because we received so many excellent manuscripts we have decided to identify three sub-themes—one for each of the double issues. All will deal with Type II applications, but this first special issue will be those Type II uses that are related to educational uses of the Internet, the second will be papers that deal with classroom integration of technology, and the last will be articles that are project reports or articles that do not fit either of the other two categories.

As we have read the excellent papers we have received, we have reflected on the old cliché that *the more things change, the more they stay the same*. It is the greatest of understatements to say that both technology and public education have changed since the early eighties when we first conceived of the concept of Type I and Type II applications. Yet, the concept has survived and seems as applicable to many of us as it did when we first conceived of it. Perhaps that is because categorizing human activities into one group that *helps us continue to act in traditional ways* and another group that *helps us to act in new ways* is one valid approach to thinking about a far wider range of human endeavor than that which is common only to education. Perhaps it has intellectual appeal as a way to think about information technology in education because we recognize the Type I/Type II dichotomy in the activities, methods, and artifacts we encounter in everything from our daily personal lives to our professional activities. Certainly it seems to have some relevance to fields as divergent as politics, art, religion, science, mathematics, business, and a host of others, including education. Then too, although obviously simplistic, it may be one way to account for some of the conflict in our own lives as well as in the affairs of organizations and even in relations among nations. Perhaps the tension between tradition and innovation is simply a natural and inevitable part of the human condition.

In any case, the concept of Type I/Type II applications of information technology in education is one that has attracted a distinguished group of educators who have produced an impressive number of thoughtful articles. We will bring you those articles in *Computers in the Schools* in the months to come.

REFERENCES

Maddux, C.D. (1984). Educational microcomputing: The need for research. *Computers in the Schools, 1*(1), 35-41.

Maddux, C.D. (1986). Issues and concerns in special education microcomputing. *Computers in the Schools, 3*(3/4), 1-19.

Maddux, C.D., & Cummings, R.W. (1987). Equity for the mildly handicapped. *The Computing Teacher, 14*(5), 16-17; 49.

Maddux, C., & Cummings, R. (1986). Educational computing at the crossroads: Type I or Type II uses to predominate? *Educational Technology, 26*, 7, 34-38.

Maddux, C.D., Johnson, D.L., & Willis, J.W. (1992). *Educational computing: Learning with tomorrow's technologies.* Needham Heights, MA: Allyn & Bacon.

Maddux, C.D., Johnson, D.L., & Willis, J.W. (1997). *Educational computing: Learning with tomorrow's technologies* (2nd ed.). Needham Heights, MA: Allyn & Bacon.

Maddux, C.D., Johnson, D.L., & Willis, J.W. (2001). *Educational computing: Learning with tomorrow's technologies* (3rd ed.). Needham Heights, MA: Allyn & Bacon.

Marie Iding
E. Barbara Klemm

Pre-Service Teachers Critically Evaluate Scientific Information on the World Wide Web: What Makes Information Believable?

SUMMARY. The present study addresses the need for teachers to critically evaluate the credibility, validity, and cognitive load associated with scientific information on Web sites, in order to effectively teach students to evaluate scientific information on the World Wide Web. A line of prior research investigating high school and university students' credibility judgments is presented. The authors then describe an instructional intervention in which pre-service teachers develop structured evaluation forms for their students' critical evaluation of scientific information on the Web and for teachers' determinations of cognitive load associated with Web materials to be used with students. Pre-service teachers' determinations of factors associated with cognitive load include several factors not previously described in other research. Finally, the authors provide recommen-

MARIE IDING is Associate Professor, Department of Educational Psychology, College of Education, University of Hawaii, Honolulu, HI 96822 (E-mail: miding@ hawaii.edu).
E. BARBARA KLEMM is Professor, Department of Curriculum Studies, College of Education, University of Hawaii, Honolulu, HI 96822 (E-mail: klemm@hawaii.edu).

[Haworth co-indexing entry note]: "Pre-Service Teachers Critically Evaluate Scientific Information on the World Wide Web: What Makes Information Believable?" Iding, Marie, and E. Barbara Klemm. Co-published simultaneously in *Computers in the Schools* (The Haworth Press, Inc.) Vol. 22, No. 1/2, 2005, pp. 7-18; and: *Internet Applications of Type II Uses of Technology in Education* (ed: Cleborne D. Maddux, and D. LaMont Johnson) The Haworth Press, Inc., 2005, pp. 7-18. Single or multiple copies of this article are available for a fee from The Haworth Document Delivery Service [1-800-HAWORTH, 9:00 a.m. - 5:00 p.m. (EST). E-mail address: docdelivery@haworthpress.com].

Available online at http://www.haworthpress.com/web/CITS
© 2005 by The Haworth Press, Inc. All rights reserved.
Digital Object Identifier: 10.1300/J025v22n01_02

dations for effective instruction in critical Web information evaluation for educators and students in this important aspect of critical scientific literacy. *[Article copies available for a fee from The Haworth Document Delivery Service: 1-800-HAWORTH. E-mail address: <docdelivery@haworthpress.com> Website: <http://www.HaworthPress.com> © 2005 by The Haworth Press, Inc. All rights reserved.]*

KEYWORDS. Education, Web, critical evaluation, science, collaboration, pre-service teachers, Web site evaluation, cognitive load

What makes scientific information on the World Wide Web believable? As teachers incorporate multiple information sources in instructional contexts and as students' research becomes increasingly Web-based, more non-refereed material is brought into classrooms and incorporated into student research projects. What critical evaluation skills are necessary for sifting the plausible or credible from the misconstrued or ill conceived?

This research addresses the need for teachers to learn to critically assess the informational and cognitive load aspects of scientific information on Web sites, and to effectively teach students to evaluate information on the Web. The need for students' accurate scientific assessment of information on the World Wide Web is an issue familiar to teachers and teacher educators at all levels, especially when encountering student research that incorporates unfamiliar references from the Web. Furthermore, it is a critical need for the general public, who increasingly rely on the Web for scientific information, especially related to health care issues.

A second issue related to Web resource selection is a need for educators to make adequate determinations of cognitive load associated with Web sites. *Cognitive load* refers to the degree to which cognitive resources are engaged in by tasks related or unrelated to learning in attempting to process instructional materials (Chandler & Sweller, 1991; Sweller & Chandler, 1994). The prototypical example of an increased cognitive load that is detrimental to learning would be associated with a textbook with a related illustration or figure that is referred to on another page, requiring the reader to engage in additional cognitive resources in coordinating information from the separate information sources. On the Web, an analogous situation could involve the coordination of information on many different windows, or the presence of pop-ups (for a review of research related to multimedia, see Iding, 2000).

Issues of critical evaluation of Web resources and determinations of cognitive load are related to Maddux, Johnson, and Willis's (2001) discussion of Type II educational technology applications that improve teaching and learning in ways that would be impossible or very difficult without the technology. Web-based multimedia resources that enable users to visualize or understand scientific phenomena can be considered Type II applications. As Type II educational applications in science and other areas become more central to education and research, educators must exercise critical evaluation skills to make determinations of resource credibility as well as efficacy of instructional formats. This is especially important as educators select instructional material from the Web, and teach their own students critical evaluation skills.

CREDIBILITY OF WEB INFORMATION

In our first study in this area (Klemm, Iding, & Speitel, 2001), we compared pre-service teachers' and scientists' evaluations of 31 different scientific information sources, including popular science magazines and news magazines, museum resources, information on the Web, and television news magazines about science. Differences emerged, with the scientists being much more critical of many of the information sources than pre-service teachers. Results also indicated that high school pre-service science teachers were more like scientists than pre-service elementary teachers in their credibility judgments of information sources. This may be due to high school teachers having taken many more science classes. For example, elementary pre-service teachers rated the following categories as their top five in credibility: "resources from a museum, aquarium, or nature center" and "popularized science magazines (e.g., *Discover*)," "weekly news magazines (e.g., *Times, Newsweek*, etc.)," "CNN Cable News Network," and "TV News magazine (e.g., *20/20* or *Dateline*)." With the exception of popularized science magazines (which scientists rated in seventh place), scientists gave all of the popular news media mentioned above low credibility ratings. Instead, scientists rated a scientist researching a particular topic as most credible, followed by university extension resources, museum and aquarium resources, and PBS TV. Secondary science teachers rated aquarium and museum resources, as well as university cooperative extension resources, as tied for first place.

In response to a need for instruction in this area, we worked with high school biology students to develop criteria for critically evaluating scientific Web sites and the scientific information contained in them (Iding, Landsman, & Nguyen, 2002). Our set of criteria included credibility of authors/institutions, validity or accuracy of information, and "presentation aspects or organization of Web site[s]" (p. 376). These criteria were adapted from Rader (1998) and Farah (1995) and used in the work of Nguyen (2000). After instruction, students reported that the process of learning to critically evaluate scientific information was most valuable to them, and their lists of evaluation criteria were more extensive after instruction. Similarly, they reported that their level of confidence in their ability to evaluate information on the Web had increased and that in the future they would spend more time evaluating Web-based scientific information.

In other research, we found that university students in educational psychology classes rated their competence in evaluating information on the World Wide Web lower ($M = 3.0$ on a 5-point scale) than did computer science students ($M = 3.5$) (Iding, Auernheimer, Crosby, & Klemm, 2002). Interestingly, the reverse was true when students rated their competence in evaluating information for course-related topics. Specifically, educational psychology students rated themselves more highly ($M = 3.95$) than did computer science students ($M = 3.3$). We have argued for the need for the development of critical evaluation skills in educational contexts and discussed some of the problems faced by instructors in specific disciplines (e.g., computer science) (Iding, Crosby, Auernheimer, & Klemm, 2002).

COGNITIVE LOAD

In addition to credibility judgments, we were interested in teachers' determinations of appropriate cognitive load associated with Web sites and other multimedia materials. *Cognitive load* refers to the extent to which cognitive resources are taken up by tasks relevant or unrelated to learning (Chandler & Sweller, 1991; Sweller & Chandler, 1994). For example, to recall the prototypical illustration mentioned earlier, learners might have to allocate cognitive capacity to coordinating separate illustrations and text ("split attention effects") or processing unnecessary graphics ("redundancy effects") (Sweller & Chandler, 1994). Kischner (2002) and others (e.g., Bannert, 2002; Valcke, 2002) differentiate three types of cognitive load: intrinsic cognitive load connected with the to-be-learned material (such as reading about unfamiliar content in a second language), extraneous cognitive load associated with ineffective instructional design, and germane cognitive load related to effective learning processes (see also Van Merrienboer, Schuurman, De Crook, & Paas, 2002). An example of germane cognitive load would be a text that contains appropriate signaling devices to draw attention to major aspects of the scientific process–overviews, boldfacing of main points, and summaries.

In an era of highly touted, multimedia-rich, educational Web and text environments, we were interested in how pre-service teachers might conceptualize the notion of cognitive load in selecting appropriate Web-based materials for their students. We felt that it would be important for educators to consider that some multimedia-based learning environments possess characteristics that are more effective than others. This perspective is more closely aligned with current research than the general assumption that the more multimedia-rich a learning environment is, the more effective it must be (Iding, 2000; Iding, Auernheimer et al., 2002). To the best of our knowledge, no studies have been done involving educators' determinations of potential cognitive load.

In the present study, we describe findings from a study in which we worked with 31 pre-service teachers to develop structured evaluation forms (i.e., rubrics) for critically evaluating scientific information and cognitive load on the Web. Then, we provide recommendations for effective instruction for teacher educators, K-12 teachers, and students in these important aspects of critical scientific literacy.

METHOD

Participants

Participants were 31 pre-service teachers enrolled in two introductory educational psychology classes. Participation was voluntary and anonymous.

Materials

Each student was given a copy of a four-page set of worksheets, "Evaluating Scientific Web Sites and Science Information on the World Wide Web" that had been developed by the authors. The worksheets instructed students to:

1. Individually describe own criteria for Web site evaluation. Describe sources for criteria.
2. Read brief instruction about Web site evaluation and cognitive load.
3. In pairs, examine and evaluate actual Web sites.
4. In small groups, brainstorm and develop criteria.
5. Individually develop rubrics for students evaluating Web sites and teachers evaluating cognitive load.

Procedure

Participation took place during one class session. Students followed instructions in the worksheets for the sequence of activities. They completed the worksheets in the class sessions, partly as individuals and partly in pairs and in small groups.

The authors worked together and created categories to account for the general themes that emerged from student comments.

RESULTS AND DISCUSSION

We summarize our findings in tabular form, indicating categories selected to represent student comments and frequencies. Table 1 shows the preliminary criteria that pre-service teachers listed individually when we asked them what criteria they use when determining whether they will use or cite information from a Web site. Credibility and relevance were students' top two choices. A comprehensive criteria list provided by one student included the following: "if it's from a major

TABLE 1. Pre-Service Teachers' Criteria for Using Information from a Web Site

Criteria	f	Criteria	f
Credibility	35	Viewpoints	4
Relevance	20	Unclear	4
Evidence	13	Popularity	3
References	9	Individual Mention/Other	3
Organization	7	Parsimony	2
Usability	6	Links	2
Currency	6	Visuals/Multimedia	1

publishing company," "if the name of the source sounds familiar (i.e., encyclopedia)," "if it's from a distinguished college or university," "if the site looks and sounds professional," and, "if the site has citations and a bibliography or something that shows the facts came from a trusted source."

Two of the other participants' comments referred to whether Web site authors had carried out research in the particular area described in the Web site. In our experience, this is an area that has been rarely raised by students. It appears that having students consider the differences between Web sites that present or cite original work (i.e., "primary sources" or "first hand," as the students describe) and Web sites that merely present "secondary information," much like many introductory textbooks, may indicate an area for further instruction.

When asked where they learned these criteria, and who taught them, most responded that they learned them on their own (17 responses); through college classes or from professors (15); from schools or teachers (6); or from other sources (2). These responses are interesting, because according to the work of Nguyen (2000), high school teachers frequently assume it is the responsibility of other teachers (usually English teachers) to have taught students critical evaluation skills. Yet, it is the experience of the first author that the majority of university students in education classes are not familiar with notions of refereeing, as it relates to refereed journal articles or scientific information. Additionally, in other research, Iding, Crosby et al. (2002) found that many college students had difficulty understanding the notion of Web site authors' potential vested interests, especially with respect to educational Web sites, which were presumed by some to be devoid of potential vested interests because they were educational.

In the next part of the activity, students worked in pairs to evaluate the credibility and validity of actual Web sites. Some of the themes that were associated with credible Web sites included lots of good information, recent, and government site. In contrast, themes that emerged from descriptions of non-credible sites included questions about authorship, not being up to date, too much information, and lack of organization. Interestingly, some of the same Web sites that were determined to be credible by some were described as not credible by others. For example, http://www.nasa.gov was described as credible by many, although one student described it as one with credibility/validity problems. This student reasoned that the Web site was limited by "not enough explanation," which seems to indicate a misconception about the nature of credibility and validity.

Factors like being up to date and containing lots of good information were associated with credibility, although how the determination of whether the information is "good," especially in areas where users have limited expertise, was not explained. Government sites, like their educational counterparts, were associated with high levels of credibility, as it appears that they are associated with objectivity and possibly the absence of vested interest, an area that might be contested strongly by Americans critical of government policies and positions and non-U.S. users.

Characteristics of non-credible Web sites were also interesting. Too much information contributed to lower credibility judgments (which appears to echo the student's criticism of the NASA Web site). Other characteristics that were associated with lower credibility included criticisms that one could also expect from scientists or other experts, such as not being up to date, lack of organization, and questionable authorship.

Next, we asked participants to develop their own structured evaluation forms/rubrics for Web site evaluation that could be used by their students (see Table 2). It is interesting that credibility and relevance remain the top two criteria (similar to their individual lists). Unlike their individual lists, usability and organization are mentioned more frequently than references and evidence, which are arguably more closely tied to credibility. The presence of other viewpoints could be seen as associated with evaluating Web sites for the presence of more objective, or less biased information.

One sample criteria list included: "the amount of grammatical errors in [the] Web site," "organization and layout," "amount of citations," and "credentials that author, Web site has." The following questions were also part of this list: "Are there any biases?" "What is the level of credibility?"

TABLE 2. Pre-Service Teachers' Criteria for Students Evaluating Web Sites

Criteria	f	Criteria	f
Credibility	27	Viewpoints	5
Relevance	18	Individual Mention/Other	4
Usability	12	Links	3
Organization	12	Unclear	2
References	9	Parsimony	1
Evidence	8	Visuals/Multimedia	1
Currency	7		

Another sample criteria list included the following: "Is there a credible author listed on the page?" "Is there a date on the page?" "Does the Web site list other sources that they received their information from?" "Is the Web site easy to use" "Is it easy to read?" In examining these lists, it is noteworthy that in working collaboratively with actual Web sites, participants noticed other aspects related to Web site evaluation that they had not mentioned earlier. For example, they noticed the presence of grammatical errors.

Next, we asked pre-service teachers to develop structured evaluation forms that would be appropriate for teachers critically evaluating cognitive load associated with Web sites. In Table 3, we summarize the criteria mentioned. In the lower part of the table are criteria that were listed that related to credibility and validity, rather than cognitive load. We also list new criteria that could be seen as relating directly to cognitive load, such as developmental appropriateness, information load, and visual density. These students were able to come up with aspects of cognitive load that appear to be very useful and appropriate, especially for this educational application of what may seem at times to be a rather abstract cognitive construct. For example, motivational aspects are not related to cognitive load in the research literature, but surely motivational/affective dimensions of learning can affect perceptions of cognitive load, if not the load itself. It is important to remember that cognitive load is partly a function of the materials, instructional formats, and tasks themselves, and partly a function of individual learners with different levels of development and expertise with respect to different kinds of content.

TABLE 3. Criteria Pre-Service Teachers Propose for Evaluating Cognitive Load of Web Sites

New Criteria	f	Criteria Related to Previous Lists	f
Developmentally/Cognitively Appropriate	15	Organization	10
Information Load	10	Relevance	7
Visual Density (Too Many/Not Enough)	7	Credibility	6
Motivating (Fun/Interesting)	4	Individual Mention/Other	6
Interactivity/Multimedia	3	Evidence	5
Visual Efficacy	3	References	4
Visual Appropriateness	2	Usability	3
Text/Visual Relationship	2	Currency	1

Table 4 incorporates two examples of pre-service teachers' rubrics, in addition to other criteria mentioned by students. Given the brevity of instruction in this area, we believe that students came up with useful criteria for teachers evaluating cognitive load.

CONCLUSION: RECOMMENDATIONS

In this study, we examined pre-service teachers' determinations of criteria for Web site evaluation and selection with respect to science content. We designed a brief instructional intervention in which pre-service teachers devised rubrics on critical Web information evaluation and on cognitive load related to Web sites.

Given the lists of criteria that participants created, we believe our instruction was successful. However, we have several recommendations to improve future instruction and research in this area:

TABLE 4. Sample Lists of Criteria Pre-Service Teachers Propose for Evaluating Cognitive Load

---

Sample Criteria List 1
- Is there an overload of information being presented?
- Are the visuals used to enhance the text presented?
- Do the graphics take over the Web page?
- Are there a lot of media techniques used?
- Is the information organized and clearly presented?

Sample Criteria List 2
- Is the information organized and easy to understand?
- Is the Web site appropriate to the reading level of the age group?
- Is the Web site easy to navigate?
- Does the Web site contain too many advertisements?
- Is the Web site appropriately interesting to the students?

Other Criteria Mentioned
- Is anything distracting (pop-up windows, links)?
- Is there any unnecessary information?
- Does the site meet the needs of visual, audio, and/or kinesthetic learners equally? If not, which does it favor/alienate? How?

---

1. Web site evaluation criteria should be explicitly taught in teacher education programs and K-12 classrooms, across the curriculum. Rather than short-term interventions, we advocate implementation throughout the school year, in many contexts. The present study and our other research in this area (e.g., Iding, Crosby et al., 2002) indicate that a need for instruction in this area remains, even in higher education.

2. We believe that teachers need to learn to make some determinations of cognitive load associated with Web sites as part of their learning critical Web evaluation skills. This is particularly important in an era where prevailing beliefs and marketing attempts implicitly promote the idea that "more multimedia is better," although research indicates that this assumption may not be completely accurate (Iding, 2000; Iding, Auernheimer et al., 2002).

3. As educators, it may be advantageous to arrive at a consensus about criteria for Web evaluation and develop terms or agreed-upon language with examples for students. Since many contemporary issues that serve as the basis for problem-based or authentic learning are contextualized and interdisciplinary, it would be useful to identify common critical evaluative criteria that cut across subject areas.

In conclusion, we note that this area related to the development and use of Web evaluation criteria is a research area in need of further work, particularly developmentally. Additionally, as more and more of our study and work as a society becomes Web based, more of the responsibility for critical evaluation rests with users, who should be educated from elementary school on in critical information source evaluation. Working with future teachers represents a useful step in this area.

REFERENCES

Bannert, M. (2002). Managing cognitive load–recent trends in cognitive load theory. *Learning and Instruction 12*(1), 139-146.

Chandler, P., & Sweller, J. (1991). Cognitive load theory and the format of instruction. *Cognition and Instruction, 8*, 293-332.

Farah, B. (1995). Information literacy: Retooling evaluation skills in the electronic information environment. *Journal of Educational Technology Systems, 24*(2), 127.

Iding, M. (2000). Is seeing believing? Features of effective multimedia for learning science. *International Journal of Instructional Media, 27*(4), 403-415.

Iding, M. K., Auernheimer, B., Crosby, M. E., & Klemm, E. B. (2002). Users' confidence levels and strategies for determining Web site veracity. *Proceedings of The WWW 2002: The Eleventh International World Wide Web Conference*, 1-3. Retrieved October 21, 2001, from http://www2002.org/CDROM/poster/index-byauthor.html

Iding, M. K., Crosby, M. E., Auernheimer, B., & Klemm, E. B. (2002). Critical evaluation skills for Web-based information: "Lies, damned lies" and Web-based information. *Proceedings of the ED-MEDIA 2002: World Conference on Educational Multimedia, Hypermedia & Telecommunications*, 269-270. Retrieved October 21, 2001, from http://www.aace.org/di/

Iding, M., Landsman, R., & Nguyen, T. (2002). Critical evaluation of scientific Web sites by high school students. In D. Watson & J. Anderson (Eds.), *Networking the Learner: Computers in Education: Seventh IFIP World Conference on Computers in Education Conference Proceedings* (pp. 373-382). Dordrecht, Netherlands: Kluwer.

Kirshner, D. (2002). Cognitive load theory: Implications of cognitive load theory on the design of learning. *Learning and Instruction, 12*(1), 1-10.

Klemm, E. B., Iding, M., & Speitel, T. (2001). Do scientists and teachers agree on the credibility of media information sources? *International Journal of Instructional Media 28*(1), 83-91.

Maddux, C. D., Johnson, D. L., & Willis, J. W. (2001). *Educational computing: Learning with tomorrow's technologies* (3rd ed.). Needham Heights, MA: Allyn & Bacon.

Nguyen, T. T. (2000). *OASIS: Student evaluation methods for World Wide Web resources*. Unpublished master's thesis, University of Hawaii, Honolulu, Hawaii.

Rader, H. (1998). Library instruction and information literacy. *Reference Service Review, 26*(3/4), 143.

Sweller, J., & Chandler, P. (1994). Why some material is difficult to learn. *Cognition and Instruction, 12*(3), 185-233.

Valcke, M. (2002). Cognitive load: Updating the theory? *Learning and Instruction, 12*(1), 147-154.

Van Merrienboer, J. J. G., Schuurman, J. G., de Croock, M. B. M., & Paas, F. G. W. C. (2002). Redirecting learners' attention during training: Effects on cognitive load, transfer test performance and training efficiency. *Learning and Instruction, 12*(1), 147-154.

Janice M. Hinson

Investigating the Perceptions and Behaviors of Elementary Students and Teachers When Internet Access Is Universal

SUMMARY. This study presents a preliminary investigation into changes in the perceptions and behaviors of teachers and students when all have universal Internet access at home and school using Internet-on-TV technology. Four hundred fourth-grade students and their teachers from seven schools participated in the WISH TV^{SM} (WorldGate Internet School to Home) Project. Through the use of qualitative research methodology, results indicated that teachers' perceptions of the benefits of Internet use and the Internet-on-TV technology had a direct impact on their decisions regarding instructional delivery. Technical and instructional support also influenced teachers' willingness to integrate Web-based resources into lesson plans. Teacher behaviors also affected student use of the Internet. In classrooms where teachers implemented Web-based resources, students reported that they were doing more homework, searching for more information, and getting better grades. Reactions to the Internet-on-TV technology varied and depended on the expectations and experiences of the users. Service limitations and technical difficulties may have curtailed enthusiasm. With some upgrades,

JANICE M. HINSON is Associate Professor, Department of Educational Leadership, Research and Counseling, Louisiana State University, Baton Rouge, LA 70803 (E-mail: jhinson@lsu.edu).

[Haworth co-indexing entry note]: "Investigating the Perceptions and Behaviors of Elementary Students and Teachers When Internet Access Is Universal." Hinson, Janice M. Co-published simultaneously in *Computers in the Schools* (The Haworth Press, Inc.) Vol. 22, No. 1/2, 2005, pp. 19-31; and: *Internet Applications of Type II Uses of Technology in Education* (ed: Cleborne D. Maddux, and D. LaMont Johnson) The Haworth Press, Inc., 2005, pp. 19-31. Single or multiple copies of this article are available for a fee from The Haworth Document Delivery Service [1-800-HAWORTH, 9:00 a.m. - 5:00 p.m. (EST). E-mail address: docdelivery@haworthpress.com].

Available online at http://www.haworthpress.com/web/CITS
© 2005 by The Haworth Press, Inc. All rights reserved.
Digital Object Identifier: 10.1300/J025v22n01_03

19

however, the Internet-on-TV technology holds some promise for connecting underserved children who lack resources to connect from home in any other way. *[Article copies available for a fee from The Haworth Document Delivery Service: 1-800-HAWORTH. E-mail address: <docdelivery@haworthpress. com> Website: <http://www.HaworthPress.com> © 2005 by The Haworth Press, Inc. All rights reserved.]*

KEYWORDS. Universal Internet access, online communities, equity, alternative Internet portals, instructional change, barriers to Internet access, changes in perceptions and behaviors of teachers and students

Many of the nation's poorer children still lag behind their more affluent peers in computer use and connectivity at home. According to DeBell and Chapman (2003), authors of *Computer and Internet Use by Children and Adolescents in 2001*, socioeconomic differences continue to have a significant impact on computer and Internet use at home by children and adolescents ages 5-17. In their report, a comparison by race reveals that 77% of White children and adolescents use computers at home while only 41% of Black and Hispanic children and adolescents do so. Differences are more dramatic when comparing income levels. For example, 31% of children and adolescents living in homes with yearly income levels of $20,000 or less use computers at home as compared to 89% of those living in families with annual incomes over $75,000. DeBell and Chapman also noted that as income levels rise, so do the percentages for home use (p. 11). The percentage of all children and adolescents using computers at home also relates to the educational attainment levels of their parents. For example, only 23% of children and adolescents living in homes where parents have less than a high school education used computers at home as compared to 69% of children and adolescents living in homes where parents have some college coursework and 89% of those whose parents have graduate education (p. 13). Of the children who had computer access at home, there were no significant differences between racial/ethnic groups in terms of their use of computers to complete school assignments (p. 21).

In the same report, DeBell and Chapman describe Internet use at home by children and adolescents ages 5-17. They found that White and Asian children and adolescents living in homes with higher income levels and more educated parents used the Internet more at home than children and adolescents living in low-income homes with less educated parents (p. 22). Children and adolescents who are more likely to rely on access through schools or other locations include children and adolescents from homes where no parent has earned a high school diploma, households headed by single mothers, Spanish/monolingual households, and families with incomes below $35,000 (p. 22). When comparing income levels for all races, children and adolescents living in families with incomes of $75,000 are four times as likely to use e-mail at home than children and adolescents from families with incomes under $20,000 (p. 25). Children and adolescents living in families with incomes of $75,000 are also four times as likely to do word processing, and three times as likely to use a home computer to complete school assignments (p. 18).

DeBell and Chapman reported no differences in Internet use rates at school for White, Black, Hispanic, or American Indian children. When comparing children and adolescents who used the Internet at only one location, however, 70% of those not living in poverty connected from home as compared to 35% of students living in poverty. Approximately 30% of Black 5-17-year-olds and 25% of 5-to-17-year-olds living in poverty used public libraries to get online, while 52% connected from school, 7% from public libraries, and 5% from someone else's home.

Kleiner and Lewis (2003), authors of *Internet Access in U.S. Public Schools and Classrooms: 1994-2002*, described Internet access in public schools and classrooms. They reported that in 2002, 99% of public schools in the United States had access to the Internet. Of these, 53% of public schools made computers with Internet access available to students outside of regular school hours. Secondary schools were more likely to make the Internet available than elementary schools, and availability was lower in schools with high concentrations of students living in poverty and in schools with the highest minority enrollments (p. 9).

Educators and government leaders are concerned that many low-income school children are being excluded from the benefits of home Internet use and are working together to find ways to provide connectivity to all children. This article describes one such endeavor, the WISH TV Project, an educational initiative designed to connect children to the Internet using the Internet-on-TV technology developed by WorldGate Communications, Inc. Users accessed the service through the use of digital cable, a wireless keyboard, and a cable set-top converter box. Local cable companies absorbed the wiring costs and WorldGate provided their service at no charge. WISH TV was piloted in seven schools in the South and Midwest to demonstrate potential uses in educational settings.

This study examined changes in the instructional behaviors of teachers and students when everyone has identical Internet access at home and school and focused specifically on: the impact of access on students' academic behaviors and perceptions of themselves as learners, changes teachers make to their teaching practices when access is universal, and reactions to WISH TV as a non-standard Internet portal.

WHY IS ACCESS IMPORTANT?

There are indications that students are learning more or achieving different learning outcomes when Web-based resources are integrated into instruction. Students in Schofield and Davidson's (2003) study, for example, reported that Web use allowed them to become self-directed learners who had more control over content. Similar findings were reported by students participating in The Laptop Kids Project (U.S. Department of Commerce, National Telecommunications and Information Administration, 2000). This project focused on increasing the connectivity of 110 low-income fourth-grade students. After acquiring Web access, students said that they felt smarter, read more, and thought their study skills had improved. Parents commented that their children were more interested in learning and were getting better grades. Principals noted that more parents were participating in parent-teacher conferences and helping their children with homework.

The findings presented in *The Digital Disconnect: The Widening Gap Between Internet-Savvy Students and Their Schools* (Pew Internet and American Life Project, 2002) provided insights into how middle and high school students are using the Internet at home and school. They noted that Internet-savvy children are using the Internet as a virtual tutor, textbook, guidance counselor, notebook, and study group. Students in their study reported that most of their Internet use occurs outside of the school day because teachers are not integrating Web resources into their teaching practices and, when they do, the quality of the assignments is disappointing. The students wanted their teachers to design and implement Internet assignments that merge home and school use to increase their potential for learning. Students also recommended that teachers be provided with training and support and urged schools to increase the quality of Internet access in schools. Educators (Cunningham, 2001; Ryder & Graves, 1997; Swain & Pearson, 2001) agree and recommend that teachers construct learning environments that prepare students to process changing streams of information, construct meaning from new and existing information, evaluate the accuracy and reliability of this information, and critically develop new connections.

METHODS

The WISH TV Project

WISH TV was piloted in public schools in the South and Midwest beginning in January 2001. Approximately 400 fourth-grade students, their parents, and their teachers participated. These schools were selected by cable companies, government officials, or school district superintendents. Each student and teacher had access to WISH TV at home and in his/her classroom. Each classroom had its own Web site where teachers could post homework assignments, class announcements, discussion topics, or curricular-related Web sites. Teachers attended a three-hour training session on using the WISH TV service and integrating Web resources into instruction. Students and parents also attended an orientation to learn to use the service. A WorldGate employee directed the project and hosted weekly conference calls with designated contacts at each school. She also promoted collaborative Web-based projects between schools and served as a liaison between the schools, their respective cable television companies, and WorldGate technicians.

Participating Schools

Seven schools participated in the WISH TV Project. Schools A and B were similar in demographics. Both schools were located in small rural communities, and over 90% of the students qualified for a free or reduced lunch. Before WISH TV was implemented, less than 10% of the students had Internet service at home. Each of these schools had four fourth-grade teachers who shared a common planning period. Teachers at both schools also had on-site technical and instructional support. At each school, two teachers were experienced Internet users and two were novices.

Schools C and D were located in the same school district in a Midwestern state. Both were urban schools with free and reduced lunch rates of 31% and 63%. Prior to WISH TV, approximately 35% of the students at each school had Internet service at home. Each school had three self-contained fourth-grade classrooms. Teachers at these schools did not share a common planning period and did not have instructional or technical support on site. Only one fourth-grade teacher at School C was comfortable using the Internet, while two teachers at School D were experienced Internet users.

Schools E, F, and G were all located in a rural Midwestern school district. Schools E and F had one fourth-grade class, while School G had two. The distance between schools limited collaboration between teachers. Support also was limited by the shared duties of the principals, who also served as curriculum coordinators for the district. The average free and reduced lunch rate for this school district was 17%. Approximately 50% of the students had Internet service prior to WISH TV.

All of these schools had several things in common. All classrooms had ISDN Internet access in addition to WISH TV, while none of the schools made Internet access available to students after hours, and none lent laptops to students or supported students e-mail addresses. Only two of the 17 teachers had classroom Web sites.

Data Collection

Data were collected through structured interviews with parents, students, teachers, and principals at all seven schools. Seventeen teachers, 44 students, 28 parents, and 7 principals were interviewed. When possible, three students and their parents were interviewed from each teacher's class. The students were selected by the teachers, and participation was voluntary. Interviews were conducted after the WISH TV service had been in place for one semester. This enabled participants to compare the impact of WISH TV on themselves and others from the first semester (no WISH TV) to the second semester (WISH TV). The results were verified by the project's contacts at each school.

Students were interviewed individually or in small groups, depending on their comfort levels. They were asked to discuss changes in their academic behaviors as a result of Internet use, differences in their perceptions of themselves as learners, the impact of WISH TV on their teachers' delivery of instruction, and changes in their levels of technical competency.

Teachers and parents were interviewed individually. Teachers were asked to describe changes in students' academic progress, attitudes, and motivation and to describe changes in their own behaviors in regard to Internet use. Parents were asked about changes in their children's academic and technical behavior and changes in their children's perceptions of themselves as learners. Principals were asked to describe changes in the behaviors of teachers and students based upon the use of WISH TV.

Data Analysis

Data were analyzed using the constant comparative method (Glaser & Strauss, 1967) as a way to uncover and compare the attitudes and behavior patterns of individual WISH TV users to those in the same group (students to other students) and then to those in other groups (teachers, principals) to reveal similarities and differences. According to Lincoln and Guba (1985, p. 341) the constant comparative method involves unitizing the data and coding emerging themes and patterns. Data are then categorized and reported. In addition to using the constant comparative method, the number of participants whose responses were similar were counted, converted into percentages, and reported.

FINDINGS

Changes in Students' Behaviors

Seventy-three percent (32/44) of the students thought being able to use the Internet at home was helping them become better students. Almost half (21/44) thought they were getting better grades because they were completing assignments in greater depth. About a third of the students (15/44) also commented that they were now more motivated to do homework. Almost two-thirds (11/17) of teachers noticed that students were becoming more independent and detail-oriented learners. Some teachers commented that children were more engaged in school and were changing their perceptions of themselves as learners. Additionally, 71% of the parents (20/28) noted changes in their children's completion of homework and commented that they were helping them with assignments. Three principals also thought that students were more engaged in classroom activities and completing more assignments at home.

Seventy-five percent of the students (33/44) reported feeling more technically proficient as a result of WISH TV. Students commented that they could now send e-mail messages, participate in online discussions, and locate information on the Internet. Additionally, 6 of the 28 parents noted specifically that WISH TV was increasing their children's technology proficiency levels.

Three of the 17 teachers did not notice any changes in their students as a result of WISH TV. All three taught at schools E, F, and G where higher percentages of students had prior Internet access at home. Two of these teachers said that initially students were excited about WISH TV, but lost interest because they had little reason to use it.

Changes in Teachers' Behaviors

Almost half of the teachers (8/17) reported incorporating more Web-based resources into lessons. These teachers taught students from lower income homes (Schools A and B). About a third of the teachers routinely integrated Web sites into their lessons, while another third stumbled over their ability to find relevant sites. The remaining third were not using WISH TV on a regular basis. Those who were more interested and had support were more willing to integrate Web resources than those who were not as comfortable or as interested.

One-third of the students (15/44) reported that their teachers were asking them to search for additional information and were posting assignments on WISH TV daily, which they thought was helpful. However, 25% (11/44) reported no instructional differences from one semester to the next. Three of the seven principals also did not notice any changes in teaching patterns once the WISH TV service was installed. However, principals' attitudes may have influenced teachers' use. In schools where principals thought the use of WISH TV was important, teachers were more excited and used it more. The same holds true for schools where the principals were not as enthusiastic. In these schools, teachers complained more about the capabilities of the service and used it less.

DISCUSSION

Although the time frame for the study was relatively short (six months), interesting teaching and learning behaviors emerged. Some of the behaviors were easy to recognize, while others were more subtle and harder to interpret. The topics below reflect some insights into what happens when teachers and students have universal access, and why some of these behaviors may have occurred.

Resource-Based Learning Environments

In this study, several teachers, specifically those in schools A and B, were beginning to create resource-based learning environments (RBLEs) (Hill & Hannafin, 2001) by engaging students in projects that enabled them to use resources to manage their own learning. In both of these schools, teachers had common planning times and instructional support from the school district. At School B, however, one teacher was not ready to integrate Web resources, even though a curriculum guide with specific links had been provided for him. Realizing this, his students took it upon themselves to create their own RBLEs by using the Internet to locate information, analyze its relevancy, and report their findings. As a result, these students were developing ways to integrate Web-based resources into curricula.

Online Communities and Attitudes Toward Participation

Although teachers may not have been totally aware of their actions, those who were actively participating in the WISH TV Project were building online communities that engaged students and their parents in collaborative learning partnerships. Partnerships such as these had not been possible in any of the participating schools prior to the installation of WISH TV, because not every child had Internet access at home. In classrooms and homes where Internet access was new, interest levels and usage by teachers and students were higher. In schools where higher percentages of students had previous access, there was not as much appreciation or use of the WISH TV service. This finding is supported by the work of McKinnon, Nolan, and Sinclair (2000), who noted decreases in students' attitudes toward technology once computer use became routine. This may also hold true for experienced Internet users. In other words, experienced Internet users have already developed the skills the new users want to learn. As a result, the experienced users in this study were not as excited about Internet access, because they already knew how to use it. This may explain differences in teachers' attitudes as well, because teachers who were experienced Internet users were less enthusiastic about WISH TV than novice or intermediate users. Attitude differences for experienced users, however, may have been caused by hesitation to use a different Internet interface or by the quality of the WISH TV service in general.

Students who participated in teacher-directed activities (homework assignments, Web-based lessons) appeared to benefit from the WISH TV service more than students who were in classrooms where teachers were not using WISH TV regularly. Again, this may be attributed to parental involvement, the excitement of being a new user, or teacher interest. Additionally, in schools where principals were actively supporting the use of WISH TV, teachers were using it more despite their own levels of technical expertise.

Teacher Beliefs and Practices

Dexter, Anderson, and Becker (1999) found that computer use by teachers may be connected to beliefs about how students learn, while Ertmer (1999) links teachers' beliefs and barriers to change. According to Ertmer, first-order barriers to change are associated with resources such as equipment, and second-order barriers are related to teachers' beliefs about teaching and learning. In the present study, access, the first barrier to change, was equal and identical. Therefore, second-order barriers such as traditional perceptions of teaching and learning may have caused teachers to minimize their use of WISH TV. Although it appeared that some teachers were interested, they said that they were waiting for more opportune times to begin use (after testing, after learning more about it). Perhaps these barriers could have been eliminated if teachers had received more training and support on how to integrate Web-based resources into their teaching practices. Anderson and Harris (1997) recommend providing new users with peer mentors, identifying and supporting lead teachers at each school, and providing common planning times for new users (p. 41). Ertmer suggests that barriers to change can be eliminated if teachers have opportunities to observe models, discuss ideas, and collaborate. In future studies, it would be helpful to consider the relationship between teacher beliefs and practices and use this information to develop ways to support and sustain change.

Reactions to the WISH TV Service

Unfortunately, WISH TV did not support functions that are standard when using a computer for access (e.g., cutting, pasting, printing, saving, or downloading files). Additionally, WISH TV did not support Flash or animations, so some Web sites were not available. The service also was very slow, and it often took two minutes or longer to access a Web site once the URL had been typed into the dialogue box. There were also delays between the keyboard and the screen which frustrated users, especially when entering text-based information like login IDs or URLs. Technical support was also limited and not available after the workday ended.

Students from School A were able to use WISH TV for a second year because their cable company was willing to continue to provide service at no charge. These students had been very responsive to WISH TV as fourth-graders; however, when they moved to the middle school for their fifth-grade year, things changed. Their fifth-grade teachers did not have the professional development training or support their fourth-grade teachers had relied upon. Additionally, their teachers did not share ideas for using WISH TV. As a result, their teachers did not use it and over time, student use decreased as well. This is supported by McCreary, Ehrich, and Lisanti (2001), who found that students were not able to sustain online components without instructional support.

CONCLUSION AND RECOMMENDATIONS

Three key issues emerged from this study. First, even young children are learning to use computers. DeBell and Chapman reported in *Computer and Internet Use by Children and Adolescents in 2001* (U.S. Department of Education, National Center for Education Statistics, 2003) that about 75% of five-year-olds use computers and about 25% are using the Internet. This means that teachers who have been slow to learn or use technology are going to be compelled to create technology-rich learning environments by technically competent students. This also means that teacher training programs and professional development units in school districts must continue to address and promote coursework and training to prepare pre-service teachers and practicing teachers who are technically and instructionally ready to meet the demands of 21st century learners.

This leads directly to the second issue, current instructional practices. In many educational settings, computers are being used to reinforce mastery of basic skills. This does little to help students learn to use technology within the context of large conceptual issues. Recommendations from educators attending the Secretary of Education's Conference on *Educational Technology 2000: Measuring the Impacts and Shaping the Future* (U.S. Department of Education, 2000) included rethinking what children should know and be able to do in this digital age and encouraging teachers to develop classroom learning cultures that are open to innovation. The International Society for Technology in Education (ISTE) is also recommending that teachers develop understanding of technology uses in educational settings, stay abreast of emerging trends, and receive support to design and implement appropriate technology-rich lessons that incorporate state and national content standards (*ISTE National Educational Technology Standards*, http://cnets.iste.org/getdocs. html).

The third issue that emerged from this study relates to equity. Currently, computer and Internet use at home is not equitable among groups within our society, and Morse (2004) notes that students with limited access are facing educational disadvantages now that almost will certainly lead to economic disadvantages later. Therefore, it is imperative for educators, government officials, and industry leaders to continue to explore or refine ways to provide even the poorest children with Internet access to maximize the learning potential of all students, not just the ones that can afford it.

REFERENCES

Anderson, S. E., & Harris, J. B. (1997). Factors associated with amount of use and benefits obtained by users of a statewide educational telecomputing network. *Educational Technology Research and Development, 45*(1), 19-43.

Cunningham, C. A. (2001). Improving our nation's schools through computers and connectivity. *Brookings Review, 19*(1), 41-43.

DeBell, M., & Chapman, C. (2003). *Computer and Internet use by children and adolescents in 2001* (NCES 2004-014). Washington, DC: U.S. Department of Education, National Center for Educational Statistics. Retrieved June 2, 2004, from http://nces.ed.gov/pubs2004/2004014.pdf

Dexter, S., Anderson, R., & Becker, H. (1999). Teachers' views of computers as catalysts for changes in their teaching practice. *Journal of Research on Computing in Education, 31*(3), 221-239.

Ertmer, P. A. (1999). Addressing first- and second-order barriers to change: Strategies for technology integration. *Educational Technology Research and Development, 47*(1), 47-61.

Glaser, B. G., & Strauss, A. L. (1967). *Discovery of grounded theory: Strategies for qualitative research.* Chicago, IL: Aldine.

Hill, J. R., & Hannafin, M. J. (2001). Teaching and learning in digital environments: The resurgence of resource-based learning. *Educational Technology Research and Development, 49*(3), 37-52.

International Society for Technology in Education. *National educational technology standards project.* Retrieved June 2, 2004, from http://cnets.iste.org/getdocs.html

Kleiner, A., & Lewis, L. (2003). *Internet access in public schools and classrooms: 1994-2002* (NCES 2004-011). Washington, DC: U.S. Department of Education, National Center for Educational Statistics. Retrieved June 2, 2004, from http://nces.ed.gov/pubs2004/2004011.pdf

Lincoln, Y. S., & Guba, E. G. (1985). *Naturalistic inquiry.* Newbury Park, CA: Sage.

McCreary, F., Ehrich, R., & Lisanti, M. (2001). A social network study of online communication among elementary students and teachers with home Internet access. *Proceedings of the Human Factors and Ergonomics Society Annual Meeting, 1*, 575-579.

McKinnon, D., Nolan, C., & Sinclair, K. (2000). A longitudinal study of student attitudes toward computers: Resolving an attitude decay paradox. *Journal of Research on Computing in Education, 32*(3), 325-335.

Morse, T. E. (2004). Ensuring equality of educational opportunities in the digital age. *Education and Urban Society, 36*(3), 266-279.

Pew Internet & American Life Project. (2002). *The digital disconnect: The widening gap between Internet-savvy students and their schools.* Retrieved June 2, 2004, from http://www.pewinternet.org/reports/toc.asp?Report=67

Ryder, R., & Graves, M. (1997). Using the Internet to enhance students' reading, writing, and information-gathering skills. *Journal of Adolescent & Adult Literacy, 40*(4), 244-254.

Schofield, J. W., & Davidson, A. L. (2003). The impact of Internet use on relationships between teachers and students. *Mind, Culture, and Activity, 10*(1), 62-79.

Swain, C., & Pearson, T. (2001). Bridging the digital divide: A building block for teachers. *Learning & Leading with Technology, 28*(8), 10.

U.S. Department of Commerce, National Telecommunications and Information Administration. (2000). *How access benefits children.* Retrieved June 2, 2004, from http://www.ntia.doc.gov/otiahome/TOP/publicationmedia/how_abc/How_ABC.html

U.S. Department of Education. (2000). Secretary of Education's Conference on Educational Technolog0y: *Measuring the Impacts and Shaping the Future.* Final report. Retrieved April 25, 2002, from http://www.ed.gov/Technology/techconf/200/report.html

Betül C. Özkan

Pros and Cons of Internet2 Videoconferencing as a New Generation Distance Education Tool

SUMMARY. Internet2 is one of the newer ways of videoconferencing in American universities. Over 200 universities in the United States collaborate with each other through these high-quality Internet lines. K-12 schools and libraries nationwide have also started taking advantage of this fiber optic, high-capacity speedy network. However, the term *Internet2* still remains obscure to many. This paper addresses pros and cons of using Internet2 as a means of videoconferencing. *[Article copies available for a fee from The Haworth Document Delivery Service: 1-800-HAWORTH. E-mail address: <docdelivery@haworthpress.com> Website: <http://www.HaworthPress.com> © 2005 by The Haworth Press, Inc. All rights reserved.]*

KEYWORDS. Internet2, videoconferencing, teacher education, distance education

BETÜL C. ÖZKAN is Assistant Professor, Media and Instructional Technology Department, State University of West Georgia, Carrollton, GA 30118 (E-mail: bozkan@westga.edu).

[Haworth co-indexing entry note]: "Pros and Cons of Internet2 Videoconferencing as a New Generation Distance Education Tool." Özkan, Betül C. Co-published simultaneously in *Computers in the Schools* (The Haworth Press, Inc.) Vol. 22, No. 1/2, 2005, pp. 33-42; and: *Internet Applications of Type II Uses of Technology in Education* (ed: Cleborne D. Maddux, and D. LaMont Johnson) The Haworth Press, Inc., 2005, pp. 33-42. Single or multiple copies of this article are available for a fee from The Haworth Document Delivery Service [1-800-HAWORTH, 9:00 a.m. - 5:00 p.m. (EST). E-mail address: docdelivery@haworthpress.com].

Available online at http://www.haworthpress.com/web/CITS
© 2005 by The Haworth Press, Inc. All rights reserved.
Digital Object Identifier: 10.1300/J025v22n01_04   33

BACKGROUND

In recent years one of the most promising emerging technologies has been Internet2, even though many do not know exactly what it is, what it does, or what it can do. "Internet2 is, basically, a collaboration of over 200 United States universities, teamed up with industry and government, to develop advanced Internet technology and applications for high-end academic experimenting and research" (CNet, 2001). Oftentimes, Internet2 refers to the connectivity itself; however, it is actually the name of the nonprofit consortium of universities whose main goal is to foster today's Internet (Salpeter, 2002). The member universities pay annual fees for connectivity to the Internet2 network. The Internet2 consortium (2003) has set three major goals for Internet2: create a leading-edge network capability for the national research community, enable revolutionary Internet applications, and ensure the rapid transfer of new network services and applications to the broader Internet community.

Even though the current Internet2 mainly serves universities, there are also a small number of projects that directly target K-12 students. Minkel (2004) states that this is "largely due to the efforts of the K20 Initiative (http://k20.internet2.edu)–a group of educators who want to bring Internet2 to all learners–which has worked diligently for the past three years to connect educational institutions to Internet2. As a result, 33 states, called Sponsored Education Group Participants, now have at least some of their schools and public libraries connected to Internet2, with more to come" (p. 39).

Internet2, a high-speed Internet network, has very similar technical features to the actual Internet, particularly in terms of the data seen in the Web browser. In other words, we see both Internets working similarly on computers. However, Internet2 has some key qualities different from the older Internet and these might have critical implications for instruction. For instance, Internet2 is 15,000 times *faster* with data transfer rates in gigabits and *more reliable*, because it has safeguards to insure that data packets are delivered. One important piece of technical information is that Internet2 uses Internet Protocol version 6 (IPv6) instead of the current Internet Protocol (IPv4). The main advantage of IPv6 is that it incorporates high reliability and high capacity (Internet2, 2002). In the commercial and research circuits, IPv6 is considered to be the next generation Internet protocol, which makes possible high tech Internet applications. On the other hand, it is still possible to use the current Internet protocol, IPv4, for Internet2 connectivity, and so Internet2 does not require additional protocols. Another implication of this new protocol is that it allows applications requiring high bandwidth to coexist. Videoconferencing systems are the best examples of these applications.

Even though it is not available for every university and school today, in the near future Internet2 capabilities will spread. Internet2 is reminiscent of the first days of the actual Internet. The first host computer at the University of California at Los Angeles (UCLA) campus served certain research institutions first, and then additional universities added quickly to the network for scholarly research purposes. During the following years, the first Internet network, ARPANET, has evolved into today's Internet protocol and is open to everybody, including individuals in their homes.

RELATED TERMINOLOGY: ISDN AND H.323

Today there are many different videoconferencing tools, protocols, and network systems based on different technologies. Explaining them in detail is not the intent of this paper. However, it is useful to clarify two terms to avoid confusion about Internet2. The first term is *Integrated Services Digital Network* (ISDN). "ISDN is comprised of digital telephony and data-transport services offered by regional telephone carriers. ISDN involves the digitization of the telephone network to transmit voice, data, text, graphics, music, video, and other source material over existing telephone wires" (ISDN Glossary, 2002, p. 1). Since ISDN uses phone lines provided by phone companies, it is a relatively expensive method of videoconferencing. However, because of the ease of use and ubiquitousness of phone lines, this type of videoconferencing is often preferred by both universities and businesses.

Another term relevant for videoconferencing is *H.323*. This is an operational protocol that provides a foundation for audio, video, and data communications across IP-based networks, including the Internet. H.323 is important as it provides comprehensive and flexible multimedia products and applications through Local Area Networks (LAN), which dominate recent desktop and Internet-based videoconferencing applications. The H.323 standard allows point-to-point videoconferencing as well as multipoint videoconferencing, including stand-alone devices and personal computer devices. These features of H.323 protocol match well with Internet2, so it is widely implemented.

The purpose of this paper is to compile related literature for interested educators and discuss possible advantages and disadvantages of using Internet2-based videoconferencing in educational settings.

REVIEW OF THE LITERATURE

Petersen (2000) describes the NASA Learning Technologies Project (LTP), which has been conducting ongoing research in supplementing and enhancing K-12 science and mathematics classrooms through videoconferencing technology. A group of researchers at NASA conducts videoconferences, aligning their presentations with national content standards, and they develop pre- and post-conference activities for many of the sessions. In March 1998, they also conducted a distance learning survey, and the results showed that 60% of the respondents used videoconferencing for staff development and electronic field trips. (This survey is available at: http://www.lerc.nasa.gov/WWW/K-12/ CoE/Glenn_LTP_Distance_Learnin.htm.)

Charnitski and Harvey (2000) examined pre-service teachers' development of science concepts when learning at a distance through videoconferencing. This pilot study investigated the use of the investigation/colloquium discussions (a series of student-directed explorations with hands-on materials followed by colloquium discussions facilitated by an adult learner) by 10 students connected to one another via a videoconference system. Results of this study indicated that Vygotskian socio-cultural learning in the development of science concepts could take place effectively when the groups used videoconferencing.

Martinez and MacMillan (1998) reported a successful example of videoconferencing among students of the University of Florida (U.S.) and University of Calgary (Canada). To overcome the physical limitations of a single campus, they connected students via videoconferencing as a major vehicle of communication. The goal of the study was to allow students from both countries to interact with professors and with one another on a regular basis. Student evaluations on both campuses indicated that videoconferencing added value to the learning experience and helped to diversify student profiles.

Lee and Geller (2003) think that Internet-based learning systems are limited in terms of their ability to deal with diverse learners and diverse requirements, and the high cost and effort needed for developing a new learning system. This led them to provide an educational middleware suite called *Collaborative and Sharable Learning (CoSL)*, which can handle diverse requirements and various learning components distributed over the Internet. To meet the challenging requirements of learning systems, the CoSL system has adopted three advanced techniques: (a) Extensible Markup Language (XML)-based data exchange and integration, (b) agent-based interaction and communication, and (c) data mining-based intelligent decision making. The CoSL system allows the building and managing of global learning systems in a distributed and heterogeneous environment.

These studies show that videoconferencing is a promising, high-capacity set of applications for learning and teaching. However, issues with slower networks, limited bandwidths, or unsecured Internet systems still remain problematic, so studies that investigate videoconferencing from the Internet2 perspective are needed.

FOCUS OF THE PAPER:
HIGHER EDUCATION AND TEACHER EDUCATORS

This paper addresses some aids and cautions in the successful use of Internet2. It is obvious that Internet2 will soon be available for general use, much like what happened with the original Internet. Teacher educators and teachers who wish to make use of Internet2 will benefit from these early illustrations. Lan and Gemmill (2000) believe that higher education will continue to be proactive in the evolution of next generation networks such as Internet2. Therefore, the focus of this paper is mainly on higher education, since Internet2 originated from this level.

USE OF INTERNET2 AS A VIDEOCONFERENCING TOOL

Internet2 seeks to demonstrate the next generation of computer network applications, such as learningware, tele-immersion, digital libraries, and virtual laboratories (Lan & Gemmill, 2000). More specifically, videoconferencing is one of the most widely used Internet2 tools. In this regard, Mutch and Ventura (2003) state the following:

> The greater bandwidth allows a true two-way conversation, with broadcast-quality images, real-time audio, and very few errors and delays. In its most basic form, videoconferencing requires two videoconferencing cameras, speakers, and microphones, a few

network cables, and an Internet2 connection. Videoconferencing software like NetMeeting, to send and receive the audio and video streams, is also necessary. More advanced configurations include standalone cameras operated via remote control units and LCD projectors for the video image. (p. 14)

In universities connected to the Internet2 network, videoconferencing can serve as a collaboration tool on research projects with other universities, as well as bring together students from different sites to share knowledge and ideas. Teacher educators can also use Internet2 videoconferencing capabilities to share their expertise with those in other institutions, to teach classes, and also to bring experts from other universities to their classroom environment.

By using Internet2 videoconferencing in graduate classes, over 200 universities are able to connect with their collaborative research and teaching partners to enhance and expand what occurs in the classroom. The importance of sharing experiences and information among institutions, as well as among students at the graduate level, could be invaluable. For instance, if a university does not currently have an expert in the field of technology policy on the faculty, graduate students at the university may complete courses in this area from other universities by using Internet2-based videoconferencing. Not only does this allow faculty to employ the expertise of their colleagues, it also allows students to be exposed to different perspectives, as well as to have direct links with subject experts. On the other hand, use of Internet2 at the public school level might be problematic in that K-12 partners have access issues and problems at the moment.

ADVANTAGES AND DISADVANTAGES OF INTERNET2

In terms of the advantages of using Internet2-based videoconferencing, there is the fact that it is by far the best distance system with which one can work. In other words, the quality of the video and audio is at its best level. Those using the Internet2 system feel very much like they are all in the same room.

Another advantage is that Internet2 is a way to gain access to expertise or to form student and collegial relationships that would otherwise be much more difficult to do. For example, we can use the phone and ask someone to talk about his/her topic. If a lecture is videotaped, it also is not the same thing as having that person speak, interact, and take questions from students, make points specifically to individual students who can make points back so that it is more of a conversation than viewing a packaged lecture. However, Internet2 videoconferencing is very different from these illustrations in terms of technical quality and interactivity.

In addition, Internet2 costs nothing for the teacher preparation programs to use. Today, some states have local distance education networks for videoconferencing purposes. However, Internet2 has more flexibility in terms of location and ease of use. Also, most local networks charge large fees.

There are some limitations on videoconferencing. Videoconferencing is not the same thing as face-to-face instruction. To some teacher educators, videoconferencing might be distracting because having at least two different audiences at the same time could be confusing and result in uncertainty about who to attend to. Educators need to be aware of the fact that a face-to-face learning environment still provides the most successful option for instruction. However, the main disadvantage of Internet2 seems to be the access issue for both K-12 schools and university partners.

Another concern with videoconferencing is that some universities may use it to sell materials in which they are not skilled. One teacher educator who uses Internet2 in his regular graduate classes stated:

> Well, the danger here is being able to do it and being able to do it well are two different things. In other words, the danger is, what they say about "When you have a new hammer everything in the world looks like a nail," so having Internet2 capability may make everything in the world look like a good opportunity for a distance education course. (Willis, Jerry, personal communication May, 2003)

In summary, the main advantage of Internet2-based videoconferencing in the pre- or in-service teacher training classrooms is to gain access to expertise, build relationships among students and colleagues, and take advantage of high-quality capability. Another important advantage of this system is its cost-effectiveness. In order to have connections with distant sites, colleges of education do not have to pay anything other than phone costs. The main disadvantage of Internet2-based videoconferencing may be related to the limitations of all distance education systems: They do not provide the full advantages of face-to-face instruction.

ROLE OF INSTITUTION

The role of the institution in being part of the Internet2 consortium is critical since teacher educators do not initiate this process. This means that administrators or faculty at the university level need to purchase this technology. At the moment, the Internet2 consortium includes mostly research Title I universities, which can put money into an infrastructure and invest in people's expertise so that if there is a question or problem, somebody with some expertise can help. This gives some universities a pool of expertise from research institutions that they may otherwise lack. Besides, these research universities have more funding and grant possibilities so that even without spending from the regular university budget, the first system set up at the department level could come from other resources. Also, having distinguished undergraduate and graduate programs means that there are some students who have an interest, willingness, and some expertise and this may be considered as the contribution of the institution.

The difficulty of the institution in using Internet2-based videoconferencing is its lack of visibility. Some universities do not inform their faculty and staff members that they have Internet2 capacity and connectivity. In other words, some universities provide this opportunity to certain faculty and students without giving full information, or advertising it to the entire university. Additionally, the use of some new technologies requires technology expertise. Moreover, there are currently only 202 universities connected to the Internet2 network.

PROJECTIONS FOR THE FUTURE

Internet2-based videoconferencing definitely has the potential to be the next generation of technology for distance education. Unlike many other distance education environments whose major goal is to increase class sizes, Internet2-based videoconferencing works best with smaller groups of students. It also opens the way for new types of research and teaching entailing collaboration among higher education institutions as well as business and government.

The access issue for K-12 schools creates the main barrier to effective use in teacher education programs. Once we have this, there will be many possibilities. For example, in the K-12 setting, children reading a particular author could talk to that author and see her while having a conversation. Or, pre-service teacher education students can be connected directly with real classrooms, and real classroom teachers. In the future, staff development, mentoring, in-service teacher education programs, pre-service and in-service teacher collaborations and projects, and online workshops would be possible through Internet2 videoconferencing. The main purpose here is bringing expertise into K-12 schools and breaking down some of the walls and barriers that tend to isolate our schools from the outside community and expertise. A way has to be determined to provide access for K-12 schools, but the capacity is not quite sufficient at this point.

In conclusion, the use of Internet2-based videoconferencing is one of the most powerful emerging technologies in teacher education programs. Although at this point, Internet2 is only available to a limited number of institutions, it is expected that the technology will be available to everyone in the near future, and it will likely become less expensive, higher quality, smaller in size, and more powerful.

When Internet2 expands to public schools, community colleges, museums and libraries, it will enhance the possibility of streaming videoconferencing and other applications. There are already some important initiatives: The International Society for Technology in Education (ISTE), the Consortium for School Networking (CoSn), and Educause are only a few of the groups involved in several educational projects for Internet2. There is also the Internet2 consortium, which is initiating K-12 university partnership projects in more than 20 states. (For more information about these initiatives, go to the Internet2 K-20 Initiative Web Site, Current Projects and Partnerships: http://www.internet2.edu/k20/currentprojects/index.shtml.) This also means that adapting these applications to the needs of K-12 institutions will require some work, not only in technical or financial terms, but pedagogically too. We need to be aware of the fact that Internet2 is only a new tool. As in the use of other information technologies, it needs pedagogical groundwork.

Another important development regarding Internet2 is establishing ties with overseas partners through mutual agreements and enabling collaboration between the United States and other countries around the world. These collaborations have already started among research institutions from different parts of the world, and more information about these projects and countries can be found at Internet2 consortium's Web page: http://www.internet2.edu/international/index.html.

REFERENCES

Charnitski, C. W., & Harvey, F. A. (2000, October). *Learning science concepts at a distance in pre-service teacher education: Results of a pilot study.* Paper presented at the National Convention of the Association for Educational Communications and Technology, Denver, CO. (ERIC Document Reproduction Service No. ED455764)

Cnet Builder. (2001). *Solutions for Web builders.* Retrieved October 15, 2003, from http://builder.cnet.com/webbuilding/pages/Servers/Internet2/ss01a.html.

Davidson, H. (2001). Top 10 technology breakthroughs for schools: Digital video [Electronic version]. *Technology & Learning, 22*(4). Retrieved October 15, 2003, from http://www.techlearning.com/db_area/archives/TL/200111/toptech5.html.

Integrated Services Digital Network. (2002). *Cisco documentation.* Retrieved October 15, 2003, from http://www.cisco.com/univercd/cc/td/doc/cisintwk/ito_doc/isdn.htm

Internet2. (2003). *Internet2 consortium homepage.* Retrieved October 15, 2003, from http://www.internet2.edu

Lan, J., & Gemmill, J. (2000). The networking revolution for the new millennium: Internet2 and its educational implications. *International Journal of Educational Telecommunications, 6*(2), 179-198.

Lee, Y., & Geller, J. (2003). A collaborative and sharable Web-based learning system. *International Journal of E-Learning, 2*(2), 35-45.

Martinez, M. D., & MacMillan, G. (1998, September). *A joint distance learning course in American government.* Paper presented at the Annual Meeting of the American Political Science Association, Boston, MA. (ERIC Document Reproduction Service No. ED428005)

Minkel, W. (May 2004). It's a bird. It's a plane. It's Internet2. *School Library Journal, 50*(5), 39.

Mutch, A., & Ventura, K. (2003, Summer). The promise of Internet2. *Library Journal, 14.*

Petersen, R. (2000). 'Real World' connections through videoconferencing–We're closer than you think! *TechTrends, 44*(6), 5-11.

Salpeter, J. (2002). Internet2: Building a better Net [Electronic version]. *Technology & Learning, 22*(7). Retrieved October 15, 2003, from http://www.techlearning.com/db_area/archives/TL/2002/02/newsextra.html.

Janaki Santhiveeran

Building Online Communication into Courses: Possibilities and Cautions

SUMMARY. The main purpose of this article is to discuss possibilities and concerns associated with building online communication into on-campus and online distance education courses. This article presents guidelines related to teaching strategies and procedures that maximize the integration of online communication in higher education. A sample of feedback regarding students' experiences with online communication is presented. Application to higher education is explored. This article is based on personal experience of the author in using a constructivist model to build online communication into 61 graduate and undergraduate courses since 1995. *[Article copies available for a fee from The Haworth Document Delivery Service: 1-800-HAWORTH. E-mail address: <docdelivery@ haworthpress.com> Website: <http://www.HaworthPress.com> © 2005 by The Haworth Press, Inc. All rights reserved.]*

KEYWORDS. Online communication, possibilities, concerns, e-mail, digital drop box, virtual chat, electronic bulletin board, higher education, on-campus courses, online distance education courses

JANAKI SANTHIVEERAN is Assistant Professor, Department of Social Work, California State University, Long Beach, Long Beach, CA 90840 (E-mail: jsanthiv@ csulb.edu).

[Haworth co-indexing entry note]: "Building Online Communication into Courses: Possibilities and Cautions." Santhiveeran, Janaki. Co-published simultaneously in *Computers in the Schools* (The Haworth Press, Inc.) Vol. 22, No. 1/2, 2005, pp. 43-55; and: *Internet Applications of Type II Uses of Technology in Education* (ed: Cleborne D. Maddux, and D. LaMont Johnson) The Haworth Press, Inc., 2005, pp. 43-55. Single or multiple copies of this article are available for a fee from The Haworth Document Delivery Service [1-800-HAWORTH, 9:00 a.m. - 5:00 p.m. (EST). E-mail address: docdelivery@haworthpress.com].

Available online at http://www.haworthpress.com/web/CITS
© 2005 by The Haworth Press, Inc. All rights reserved.
Digital Object Identifier: 10.1300/J025v22n01_05

The intent of this paper is to discuss possibilities and concerns associated with building online communication into on-campus and online distance education courses. It presents guidelines related to teaching strategies and procedures that maximize the integration of online communication in higher education. A sample of feedback regarding students' experiences with online communication is presented. Application to higher education is explored. This article is based on my own personal experience in using a constructivist model to build online communication into nearly 61 graduate and undergraduate courses since 1995.

Traditionally, teachers are viewed as providers and students as passive learners. Educational reform emphasizes changes in teaching strategies to promote collaboration, critical thinking, and problem-solving skills (Rice & Wilson, 1999; Vidoni & Maddux, 2002). Such reformers advocate for the use of technology and social constructivism to promote interaction. According to Copley (1992), constructivism emphasizes that the instructor play the role of facilitator to engage students in learning. In a constructivist model, learning is perceived as a social and collaborative activity (Willis, Steven, & Matthew, 1996; Dokter & Heimann, 1999). Over the years, this principle has guided me to build online communication into both on-campus and online distance education courses.

PRIOR LITERATURE

The Internet offers a wide array of opportunities that facilitate interaction and support the learning process. Only faculty members skilled with HTML and scripting languages were able to develop Web-based interfaces for their courses until the mid 1990s. Suddenly, there was an easy way to structure and build online communication into courses without hours of programming (Lake, 2001; McCollum, 1997; Rodgers, 2000). Web-based instruction reached mainstream faculty with the proliferation of Web-based course design software such as Web CT, Mallard, Blackboard, and WebBoard (Fredrickson, 1999; Knowles, 2000). Several products offer communication tools such as e-mail, digital drop box, electronic bulletin board (EBB), and virtual chat rooms for creating exciting, interactive, and user-friendly collaborative learning activities.

Literature has outlined possibilities and difficulties of using online communication tools. Online communication offers opportunities for quieter students to interact with their peers (Huff, 2001), offers opportunities to develop learning communities (Killian, 1994), facilitates teamwork (Lee, 1999), and promotes turn-taking and cooperative learning (Holden, 1993; McConnell, 1994; Randolph & Krause, 2002). It was found that reading and posting online messages in general facilitated learning and interaction (Randolph & Krause, 2002). Research findings show that both synchronous (virtual chat) and asynchronous (EBB) online communications enhance subsequent face-to-face discussions in higher education (Dietz-Uhler & Bishop-Clark, 2001). Communication tools did not reduce the need for the instructor's assistance. Online communication enhanced instructors' efforts to help students construct new knowledge and reconstruct existing knowledge (Wilson & Marsh, 1995).

Online communication is not a solution to all educational problems and cannot replace all types of classroom activities and communication. Size of the group as a whole or varying activity levels of members within the group affect the group process and its sustainability (Butler, 2001). Chat rooms require students to pay attention to themes and threads of discussions by linking a new message with the existing conversation (Schoech, 2000). There is only limited discussion in the literature on the benefits and limitations of online communication. Therefore, the focus of this paper is to discuss possibilities and concerns based on my personal experience of using a constructivist model in building online communication into 61 on-campus and online distance education classes since 1995.

BUILDING ONLINE COMMUNICATION INTO COURSES

Over the years, I have integrated e-mail, e-mail listserv, CGI forms, and EBB into on-campus undergraduate research methods and statistics courses. In the mid-1990s, I custom designed nine Web-based courses using HTML, scripting languages, and Web authoring software products for courses. Only later did I find course management software. Years of knowledge of hypertext markup language (HTML) and scripting languages became much less valuable with the advent of course authoring software such as Blackboard. I have divided the process of building online communication into courses into the following two phases.

Phase 1: Ease of Integrating Online Communication

I have built online communication into courses incrementally over the years. I created a Web Forum called "Ask Me!" within the "Teacher's

Corner" bulletin board to enable students to ask questions or receive clarifications at their convenience. Whenever I taught multiple sections of the same course, I developed one online discussion board. I rarely gave grades for their online class participation. Students voluntarily used online communication and felt comfortable learning to use online tools by trial and error.

I usually plan my integration of online communication using the Incremental Model of Building Online Communication (Figure 1), which I have been developing over the years. The model outlines the introduction of online media from the simplest readily available technology to advanced complex tools. In the beginning of each semester, I use e-mail to interact with students by sending welcome messages or sharing e-mail addresses. Second, I encourage students to use the digital drop box by helping them to submit their beginning assignments in my digital drop box. Third, I introduce EBB forums to promote interaction among students and between students and myself. Depending upon the students' comfort level with the use of the above media, I introduce vir-

FIGURE 1. Incremental model of building online communication.

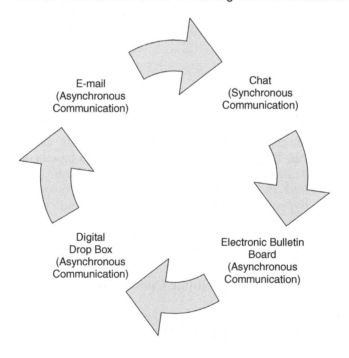

E-mail
(Asynchronous
Communication)

Chat
(Synchronous
Communication)

Digital
Drop Box
(Asynchronous
Communication)

Electronic Bulletin
Board
(Asynchronous
Communication)

tual chat for virtual office hours, consultations, and classroom discussions. Such incremental integration of online communication tools offers the opportunity for me to carefully evaluate student readiness for the next level of online communication. Using the capabilities of Blackboard, I built digital drop box, electronic bulletin board, and virtual chat into courses (Blackboard, Inc., 2004). In some classes, I have integrated only one or two communication tools depending upon student readiness, the course timeline, learning activities, and student learning styles.

Phase 2: Ease of Use of Communication Tools

One of the strengths of course management software such as Blackboard lies in its flexibility and in its ability to have full control with navigation. Students can spend as much time as desired on any of the following communication areas.

E-mail. Most of the time, students send e-mail from their preferred e-mail address. Students usually send e-mail to all the other students or select individuals from a course Web site. E-mail messages sent from the course Web site were delivered to students' e-mail addresses.

Digital drop box. Digital drop box is a communication feature of Blackboard. The digital drop box is multi-dimensional; an instructor can store and send digital files to a single student, select students, or all students. However, students only can send files to their instructors and not to other students. In addition to stamping each digital document with the date and time, the digital drop box shows the size of the document. I usually graded assignments electronically and returned the assignments with my comments to the student digital drop box. Online distance education students used digital drop box and e-mail much more than on-campus students. For example, I had 691 submissions from online distance education students for a period of two semesters from 21 students. The digital drop box feature made file sharing and archiving simple.

Electronic bulletin board forums. Group pages are simple to use in generating threaded discussions. A threaded discussion is a series of linked messages. The series is created over time as participants read and reply to existing messages (Miami-Dade Community College, 2001). Students added new threads whenever a new question was posted. For example, students sought feedback actively through the Ask Me Web forum that I created for research methods and statistics courses. Within a few days of developing online task groups, students exceeded class expectations by organizing online group meetings and posting several messages. During the same week, I noticed a new phenomenon. Interestingly, two of the most active task groups from an on-campus research methods course used threaded group forums instead of virtual chat for their synchronized group meetings. One of the groups met more than eight times on Thursday evenings, yielding 172 postings for the entire semester, meaning each student had posted nearly 25 messages outside the class. These postings are a demonstration of peer support and document that learning could occur actively beyond the traditional classroom.

Virtual chat. The use of virtual white board at Blackboard's virtual chat needs creativity. White board is used in several ways, including posting discussion questions, offering slide shows, displaying Web pages, accessing Web e-mail and drawing objects. For example, I used virtual chat for in-class group discussions by posting discussion questions and offering consultations during virtual office hours for online distance education students. Only a small number of students from each class has taken advantage of this tool as the virtual chat needed synchronized time for interaction.

Possibilities

There are endless possibilities for the instructors who believe in education reform and the constructivist model. I have identified the following benefits and presented them in a pyramid diagram called a Hierarchy of Benefits (Figure 2). The pyramid ranks the benefits from the basic to the advanced level.

Convenience! Convenience! My initial integration of e-mail into courses is mainly motivated by the convenience. Students used e-mail to get answers to their questions between class meetings. Digital drop box was mainly used by the students, as they could submit their assignments up to the last minute. Their use of virtual office hours was motivated by their interest in getting instant answers to their questions.

Increases participation. Once students became comfortable in using online communication at their convenience, I introduced activities using EBB to involve them in class discussions. EBB allowed for simultaneous, multiple conversations, or postings. Therefore, the members need not wait to take turns. The group members at EBBs posted and read messages at their convenience. Online groups encouraged more participative dynamics than did face-to-face groups. Active interaction

FIGURE 2. Hierarchy of benefits.

Possibilities

among the students facilitated the construction of knowledge, which is emphasized in a constructivist model.

Increases collaboration. Since I have created course-based EBB by merging students from multiple sections, online participation resulted in collaboration and interaction among students across class boundaries and distant sites. Due to extended interaction, students formed their own study groups, social groups, and learning communities. As suggested by a constructivist model, integration of online communication made learning a social and collaborative activity. Communication tools offered socially oriented environments for learning, which is a shift from a traditional individually centered method of teaching.

Facilitates learning, critical thinking and problem-solving. Asynchronous EBB interactions enriched the content of the course and learning experience. Students had time to provide thoughtful questions and responses. Small task groups and informal chat promoted the thinking and problem-solving capabilities of students. Learning was viewed as a process of enquiry where students became active participants in their learning. Communication tools acted as mediators for active learning to occur by solving problems and critical enquiry. Learning occurred as an active process of constructing rather than acquiring knowledge.

Facilitates task accomplishment. When students had become active in participating in online discussions and had offered support to one another, I created small task groups. Small groups facilitated accomplishment of tasks efficiently without any travel. Small task group members felt a part of the group when they knew everyone and interacted actively with their peers.

Facilitates virtual guest lectures. Once collaboration was established, I enriched the content delivery by bringing in virtual guests. For example, I invited an e-therapist from the East Coast to offer a guest lecture at a western university. The graduate students had an opportunity to ask questions and interact with the virtual guest lecturer online at their convenience using EBB.

Facilitates archiving and transferring of online discourse. Finally, I explored ways to transfer online postings from one course to the next. Luckily, Blackboard software enabled me to archive and transfer EBB postings from one semester to the next. Therefore, the resourceful discussions and virtual guest lectures were transferred to the other students learning the same course content.

Limitations and Concerns

As with any technological innovation, there are three major concerns with integrating online communication tools: systemic issues, student-centered concerns, and instructor-centered concerns (see Figure 3). Systemic issues include access, technical problems, and lack of coherence. They are related to technological capabilities of software or hardware used for online communication. Second, student concerns include lack of skills, anxiety, and frustration. They affect the students' ability to use online communication. Finally, concerns related to time and faculty workload affect the instructor's ability to promote learning.

Access and technical problems. In the beginning years, students were intimidated by the use of technology due to lack of access and technical

FIGURE 3. Concerns and guidelines.

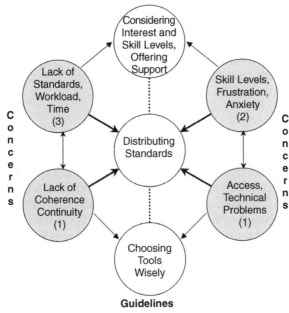

Note:
1. Systemic Issues
2. Student Centered
3. Faculty Centered

problems. Students with old computers and slow connections were perhaps the most frustrated of all. Virus transfer was a problem due to attached materials in e-mail, digital drop boxes, and EBBs.

Lack of coherence. Though virtual chat was the only communication
tool offering opportunities for real-time communication, concerns
arose. Students felt there was a lack of coherence and continuity with
online discussions using virtual chat. There was a time lag between
questions and answers, resulting in extra effort required to logically
connect questions with responses.

Frustration and anxiety. Lack of computer skills and knowledge led
to frustration. Students who were anxious and computer phobic did not
use online communication actively.

Workload and time. Another concern was related to time and faculty
workload. Although enabling and disabling online communication took
very little time, the site management and management of online discus-

sions took an inordinate amount of time. By creating several asynchronous task groups, I created a heavy workload for myself. Active groups were at times overwhelming, as they required an enormous amount of time to read and respond to on an ongoing basis.

Lack of standards. Students expected very quick responses for their postings and submissions. They were not educated sufficiently on what to expect from the instructor in terms of expected turn-around time and the instructor availability.

Guidelines

Several of the concerns identified may be avoided by thoughtful planning, careful implementation, and setting of realistic expectations. On the basis of my personal experience in developing and facilitating online communication, the following guidelines related to teaching strategies and procedures are proposed to build online communication into courses and to address the concerns discussed. These guidelines include:

1. *Choosing tools wisely.* Instructors must choose course management software or tools for online communication based on its availability, speed, faculty workload, and intended tasks.
2. *Considering student interests and skill levels.* Online groups must be formed by taking into consideration the interests and skill levels of students.
3. *Offering support.* Educators must be competent in offering support and assistance as and when needed to minimize student frustration and anxiety with using communication tools. In addition, instructors must identify and connect needy students to campus resources to facilitate and sustain student use of online media.
4. *Distributing standards.* Instructors must distribute written standards and expectations on expected turn-around time, technical requirements to use online tools, on-campus support and resources, and dos and don'ts. Instructors must facilitate thoughtful postings and help students to focus on task completion.

Student Feedback

How do I know things worked? Besides my own experience and observation, feedback from students on an ongoing basis via periodic evaluations and course evaluations is yet another strategy to evaluate the impact of building online communication into higher education. The following student comments about online communication were taken from student evaluations. These comments represent the benefits and concerns expressed by the students in their own words. They were enrolled in graduate research methods courses where I used all four communication tools that are outlined in this paper.

I feel that for many students use of computer was overwhelming, but I found it to be convenient.

She [the instructor] uses some alternative styles of teaching that are a little confusing at the beginning, but effective in the end.

This [online communication] was a frustration for me.

From the beginning she said that computer would not be the focus of the class. That clearly was not the case in this course.

A lot of students are computer and research phobic and [the instructor] goes out of her way to assure us and help us overcome fears and doubts about our abilities and aptitudes in these areas.

I believe that the instructor placed too much emphasis on the computer component, computer tasks, her own computer experimentation rather than on students' learning.

As someone who virtually never seeks help from a professor outside of class, I was amazed at the time and generosity she [the instructor] spent with me.

Thank you for the extra effort you put in to develop the computer portion of the class. I think it will assist many of our computer skills in the future.

In addition, a faculty colleague conducted focus groups to evaluate the use of technology in a research methods course. Students liked constant communication with their instructor. Students felt that the instructor was more accessible through EBB and were delighted that they could post questions at their convenience. In general, online groups offered meaningful learning experiences.

APPLICATION TO HIGHER EDUCATION

The information presented in this paper is limited in its application, since the information is based on my own personal experience and is anecdotal in nature. While the information is valuable for educators, it may not be reliable and generalizable. Nevertheless, the scope of these communication tools is broad (Flynn, 1987). Blackboard is one of the most useful course management programs for university course designers, faculty members, and trainers for building online communication into their courses. Online communication tools are useful in building chat rooms and discussion boards in many disciplines. Interviewing and counseling skills may be taught by having mock therapeutic sessions using virtual chat rooms. Communication tools would certainly enrich distance education courses, as they have the potential to offer real-time experience (Wernet & Olliges, 1998). I continue to integrate online communication into my courses as I found that the students benefit tremendously and the benefits outweigh the problems and concerns.

How would I change things if I could? Educational reform is needed in the way we teach adult learners. I welcome hybrid courses to minimize seat-based, face-to-face (F2F) learning time. Hybrid courses enable adult students to meet electronically using online communication in lieu of traditional face-to-face sessions. This will eventually promote social constructivism with improved interaction among students and creation of learning communities across county, state, and university lines.

CONCLUSION

The intent of this paper was to discuss the possibilities and concerns associated with building online communication into higher education courses. Online communication tools have the potential to promote continuity and most likely will grow at accelerating rates in the future. Online communication minimized my frustrations with several barriers for team building, online collaboration, and cooperative learning. Such constructivist values guided my integration of online communication into on-campus and online distance education courses. In order to build online communication into courses, each instructor must examine and determine whether potential benefits outweigh problems. Several of the benefits I have identified are similar to the benefits discussed in the literature. This paper elaborating on the integration of online communication tools becomes important as college graduates are expected to work in teams, to negotiate, and to collaborate. Technological innovations will characterize a host of conveniences, accompanied by a need for empirical research on the usefulness and challenges associated with online communication tools in higher education. Technological innovations are here to stay. Therefore, it is our responsibility to make online communication media work for us to promote cost-efficient collaboration, learning, and instruction.

REFERENCES

Blackboard, Inc. (2004). Welcome to Blackboard [online]. Retrieved February 4, 2004, from http://www.blackboard.com

Dokter, C., & Heimann, L. (1999). A Web site as a tool for learning statistics. *Computers in the Schools, 16*(1), 193-208.

Flynn, J. (1987). Simulating policy processes through electronic mail. *Computers in Human Services, 2*(1/2), 13-26.

Fredrickson, S. (1999). Untangling a tangled Web: An overview of Web-based instruction programs. *Technological Horizons in Education Journal, 26*(11), 67-74.

Knowles, A. (2000). Implementing Web-based learning: Evaluation results from a mental health course. Conference program and proceedings: Information Technologies for Social Work Education and Practice (CD ROM). Columbus: University of South Carolina College of Social Work.

Lake, D. T. (2001). An online formula for success. *Learning and leading with technology, 28*(6), 18-21.

Lee, C. (1999). Computer-assisted approach for teaching statistical concepts. *Computers in the Schools, 16*(1), 193-208.

Miami-Dade Community College (2001). Virtual college glossary. Retrieved February 4, 2004, from http://www.mdcc.edu/vcollege/portal/common_files/glossary.html

McCollum, K. (1997, October 31). A new industry sprouts up to help professors put courses on line. *The Chronicle of Higher Education, 44*(10), A33(2).

Rodgers, S. (2000). Blackboard overview by a technology coordinator. *Journal of Chemical Education, 77*(6), 700-701.

Schoech, D. (2000). Teaching over the Internet: Results of one doctoral course. *Research on Social Work Practice, 10*(4), 467-486.

Vidoni, K. L., & Maddux, C. D. (2002). WebQuests: Can they be used to improve critical thinking skills in students? *Computers in the Schools, 19*(1/2), 101-117.

Wernet, S. P., & Olliges, R. (1998). The application of WebCT (web course tools) in social work education. Conference program and proceedings: Information Technologies for Social Work Education and Practice (pp. 304-310). Columbus: University of South Carolina College of Social Work.

Wilson, E., & Marsh, G. (1995). Social studies and the Internet revolution. *Social Education, 59*, 198-202.

Judi Repman
Cordelia Zinskie
Randal D. Carlson

Effective Use of CMC Tools in Interactive Online Learning

SUMMARY. Instructors designing online learning can utilize an array of computer-mediated communication tools to promote student engagement and interaction. This paper surveys the tools available, focusing on uses of the tools for learning (Type II uses). Research results and implications for practice are presented for asynchronous (e-mail, listserv, discussion boards, and blogs/Weblogs) and synchronous (chat, instant messaging, and audio and video Web-based conferencing) tools. *[Article copies available for a fee from The Haworth Document Delivery Service: 1-800-HAWORTH. E-mail address: <docdelivery@haworthpress.com> Website: <http://www.HaworthPress.com> © 2005 by The Haworth Press, Inc. All rights reserved.]*

JUDI REPMAN is Professor, Department of Leadership, Technology and Human Development, College of Education, Georgia Southern University, Statesboro, GA 30460-8131 (E-mail: jrepman@georgiasouthern.edu).
CORDELIA ZINSKIE is Associate Professor, Department of Curriculum, Foundations, and Reading, College of Education, Georgia Southern University, Statesboro, GA 30460-8144 (E-mail: czinskie@georgiasouthern.edu).
RANDAL D. CARLSON is Associate Professor, Department of Leadership, Technology and Human Development, College of Education, Georgia Southern University, Statesboro, GA 30460-8131 (E-mail: rcarlson@georgiasouthern.edu).

[Haworth co-indexing entry note]: "Effective Use of CMC Tools in Interactive Online Learning." Repman, Judi, Cordelia Zinskie, and Randal D. Carlson. Co-published simultaneously in *Computers in the Schools* (The Haworth Press, Inc.) Vol. 22, No. 1/2, 2005, pp. 57-69; and: *Internet Applications of Type II Uses of Technology in Education* (ed: Cleborne D. Maddux, and D. LaMont Johnson) The Haworth Press, Inc., 2005, pp. 57-69. Single or multiple copies of this article are available for a fee from The Haworth Document Delivery Service [1-800-HAWORTH, 9:00 a.m. - 5:00 p.m. (EST). E-mail address: docdelivery@haworthpress.com].

Available online at http://www.haworthpress.com/web/CITS
© 2005 by The Haworth Press, Inc. All rights reserved.
Digital Object Identifier: 10.1300/J025v22n01_06

KEYWORDS. Online learning, computer-mediated communication, interaction, synchronous, asynchronous, e-mail, listserv, discussion boards, chat, instant messaging, audioconferencing, videoconferencing

INTRODUCTION

As online and hybrid course offerings increase, interest in the computer-mediated communication (CMC) tools that facilitate online learning also increases. Good Type I tools simplify and automate many previously tedious and/or problematic tasks. These tools also offer considerable potential as Type II tools. Type II tools can deeply engage students in a variety of critical interactions, including learner-content interactions, learner-faculty interactions, and learner-learner interactions (Moore, 1989). This paper presents an overview of these tools in two groups. The first group includes asynchronous tools such as e-mail, listserv, discussion boards, and blogs/Weblogs. Synchronous tools, including chat, instant messaging, and audio and video Web-based conferencing, are the second group of CMC tools examined. Online course management systems incorporate some or all of these tools but the discussion presented assumes that issues related to the use of CMC transcend the use of specific management systems.

DEFINING INTERACTION IN ONLINE LEARNING

Many models have been proposed to define and describe the nature of interaction in learning. Hirumi (2002) offered a basic definition: "Each of the events associated with an instructional strategy may be considered an interaction, a transaction that occurs between the learner and other human or non-human resources" (p. 22). Moore's (1989) classification of interactions into learner-content, learner-faculty, and learner-learner interactions provides a flexible system for examination of CMC tools. Jung, Choi, Lim, and Leem (2002) applied Moore's classification system in a study of Web-based interaction. They suggested three types of interaction: academic interaction, collaborative interaction, and interpersonal or social interaction.

Research examining the relationship between interaction and student learning in online classes frames this discussion. Bannan-Ritland (2002) used meta-analysis to generate a list of 19 research outcomes. Key findings include:

1. Peer participation and instructor feedback are perceived as significant elements of interactivity;
2. High levels of interaction need to be modeled by the instructor for students;
3. Different technologies can support different kinds of instructional activities (or interactions); and
4. The instructor's role is significant in promoting interactivity and indicates a change in role from face-to-face instructional contexts. (p. 172)

These findings indicate that instructors must be familiar with the full range of CMC tools available and make strategic decisions when matching the tool with the task.

ASYNCHRONOUS CMC TOOLS

E-Mail

E-mail defined. An e-mail is a simple electronic text message that allows communication to take place independent of time or place (Jung et al., 2002). Messages can be sent from an instructor to an individual learner or to a group of learners; likewise, learners can communicate with the instructor or with fellow learners.

Educational uses of e-mail. Instructors can use e-mail to provide information about class logistics, answer questions about assignments, send assignments by attachment, respond to requests for grades, and acknowledge any messages received (Johnson & Huff, 2000). Honeycutt (2001) noted the benefits of e-mail for online peer response to other students' writing, while Vonderwell (2003) found e-mail effective in motivating undergraduate education students.

Advantages of e-mail. E-mail requires minimal computer literacy (Johnson & Huff, 2000), and the attachment feature allows students to submit assignments privately and efficiently (Tiene, 2002). E-mail allows instructors to provide immediate feedback to students (Eastman & Swift, 2002; Ng, 2001). Graduate students in a study by Johnson and Huff noted that e-mail technology made the instructor seem more accessible. Vonderwell's (2003) undergraduate students liked the fact that the online environment provided greater opportunity for asking the instructor questions.

Disadvantages of e-mail. Use of e-mail can result in a very teacher-centered approach to instruction (Ng, 2001). The accessibility of the instructor via e-mail also creates a disadvantage in that students become dependent upon instructors to provide information about the course, information that is sometimes already readily available to students on the course Web site (Vonderwell, 2003).

Things to consider. Ng (2001) stated that the instructor must clearly specify expectations or requirements related to use of e-mail within the online course. Vonderwell (2003) noted that instructors should not answer questions from students in instances where students should be able to locate the answers themselves.

Listserv

Listserv defined. Listserv is an early e-mail-based application that has been used extensively for collaboration and interaction. Listservs are established by a listowner, who may also serve as a moderator. Messages posted to the list are distributed to all members via e-mail. Most Web-based course management systems do not include listserv as an instructional tool.

Educational uses of listservs. Tiene (2000) studied use of a listserv as an extension of face-to-face class discussions. Graduate students found the listserv to be a convenient method of asynchronous communication, although they did not want to eliminate face-to-face discussions. Listservs have a history of use by higher education faculty as collaborative, current awareness tools and these uses can be replicated in online classrooms (Hyman, 2003).

Advantages of listservs. Listserv is easy to use. Habitual e-mail users may respond to discussions quickly since messages are sent directly to the user's e-mail account. Hyman (2003) reviewed research focusing on listserv use in scholarly discussion groups. He noted that "ListServ has been the great equalizer, allowing all parties to speak in the same manner, regardless of their level of technology and bandwidth access" (p. 23).

Disadvantages of listserv. Listserv messages will be received in the user's regular e-mail account, which may be overloaded with e-mail and spam. Without the structure of a threaded discussion, off-topic posts may dominate listserv messages. Listserv messages may be seen as impermanent and quickly deleted (Hyman, 2003).

Things to consider. The level of commitment required of the listowner/moderator is an important consideration. Listserv messages should be archived, especially if participation is a graded activity. Instead of establishing a class listserv, students could subscribe to an existing listserv.

Discussion Boards

Discussion boards defined. Also known as threaded discussions, forums, class bulletin boards or conferences, discussion boards are key elements in online course management systems. Different threads (or topics) may be established by instructors or students. Course management systems archive the threads (usually until deleted by the instructor) and track student use of discussion boards.

Educational uses of discussion boards. In many online classes, the discussion board is the primary tool used to facilitate interaction. Group work, such as case or project-based instructional activities, offers a natural match for discussion boards (Angeli, Valanides, & Bonk, 2003; Bender, 2003). Discussion boards can also be used for role-playing, exchange of written work, debates, sharing of resources such as course-related Web sites, and interaction with guest experts (Bender, 2003).

Advantages of discussion boards. Lapadat (2002) suggested that synchronous CMC tools pose significant limitations such as linearity, brevity, and shallowness. From her research, Lapadat concluded that "the process of participating in asynchronous online conferences enhances literate forms of higher order thinking in specific ways" (Thinking by Writing in Asynchronous Conferences section, ¶ 1). For a variety of reasons (language barriers, self-confidence, etc.) many learners never participate in face-to-face class discussions. Discussion boards are flexible tools that allow for a variety of instructional strategies (Bender, 2003; Hirumi, 2002).

Disadvantages of discussion boards. Hughes and Hewson (2001) suggested that CMC tools like discussion boards and e-mail fail to capture much of the richness of face-to-face communication. Other research indicated that deep learning or critical thinking does not naturally occur with discussion boards (Angeli et al., 2003). Many students fail to participate in threaded discussions (Bender, 2003; Chen & Hung, 2002). Assessing discussion board participation can be challenging (Bender, 2003; Knowlton, 2003).

Things to consider. Hirumi (2002) stressed the importance of following systematic instructional design processes in identifying effective uses of Type II CMC tools. Based on his own experience, Peirce (2003) stressed the importance of designing questions that "provoke discomfort, unsettle confirmed notions, uncover misconceptions, inspire curiosity, [and] pose problems" (p. 314).

Blogs/Weblogs

Blogs/Weblogs defined. A Weblog or blog is an informal personal or professional journal published on the Web. It is typically updated frequently. Each entry may contain a title, short description, the name of the author, and the date posted. Advanced content may be added in the form of text, URLs, pictures and graphics, audio and/or video, or other files. Creators and users of blogs (called "bloggers") can access the Weblog from anywhere that they can access the Web. Additionally, many blogs are available to others in the form of RSS (Real Simple Syndication or Rich Site Summary) feeds. RSS is used with blogs to allow the reader to subscribe to current, content-focused channels of information (Murphy, 2003).

Educational uses of blogs/Weblogs. Blogs can be used as online student portfolios or filing cabinets to store assignments or projects. They can be class portals where teachers keep homework assignments, links, handouts, or syllabi. They can serve as collaborative writing spaces where students share ideas and work together to jointly express ideas. Blogs have served as reader's guides for literature study, as newspapers, or as project sites where students contribute the content. Weblogs enable the user to manage the knowledge that the community assembles–in fact, they have been proposed as cheaper alternatives to course management systems (Richardson, 2004).

Advantages of blogs/Weblogs. The open, flexible nature of blogs encourages dialog among the discussion participants. When faculty invite experts in the field to participate, students are able to connect their classroom to the real world. This has a positive effect on the students who recognize that they are writing for a community much larger than the class itself (Richardson, 2003). Mitchell (2004) suggested that Weblogs are a dynamic source of content as opposed to the static sources contained in most current publications.

Disadvantages of blogs/Weblogs. Educators have been slow to adopt Weblogs for reasons of privacy, security, and access. The flexible, informal nature of blogs can also be a disadvantage in terms of maintaining focus and fostering deep, critical thinking. Blogs/Weblogs, like listserv, require the use of software not commonly included in online course management packages.

Things to consider. Use of blogs/Weblogs is still new so for many users there will be a learning curve. Harrsch (2003) suggested that collaborative learning is enhanced by the formation of smaller interest groups within a larger distributed system, with each participant being a member of several smaller, overlapping interest groups. This complex structure might be confusing to both instructors and students.

SYNCHRONOUS CMC TOOLS

Chat

Chat defined. Chat is a form of synchronous text-based communication that can occur among many individuals (Anderson, 1999). Chat rooms allow students and instructor to meet electronically at the same time, no matter where they are (Eastman & Swift, 2002). Typed messages can be seen by all persons in the chat room, who then have an opportunity to respond (Kittleson, 2002). Online course management systems typically allow chat sessions to be recorded for later viewing.

Educational uses of chat. Uses can range from course "business" tasks such as holding virtual office hours, clarifying questions and assignments, and addressing technology problems (Gonzales & de Montes, 2001) to instructional activities, including sharing examples (McKeage, 2001), brainstorming and problem solving (Ingram, Hathorn, & Evans, 2000), and reflecting on field experiences (Burnett, 2003; Kirk, 2000).

Advantages of chat. Chat creates an immediacy of communication (much like a class discussion) (Ingram et al., 2000), and chat rooms are effective for both learner-learner and faculty-learner interaction (Eastman & Swift, 2002; Wang & Newlin, 2001). Specific advantages for students include increased connectedness to the instructor and course (Wang & Newlin, 2001), greater development of social relationships and class culture (Im & Lee, 2003/2004; Kirk, 2000), and more active involvement in their learning (Eastman & Swift, 2002).

Disadvantages of chat. The specific technical requirements for the chat function (e.g., java-enabled computer), Internet disconnections, and slow response times often affect participation (Farrior & Gallagher, 2000; Tiene, 2002). In addition, Branon and Essex (2001) noted that many students lack the requisite typing skills needed for timely communication. Chat sessions often produce disjointed conversations and/or multiple conversations that students find difficult to follow (Gonzales & de Montes, 2001; Kittleson, 2002; Tiene, 2002). This problem becomes magnified when the chat group becomes too large (Branon & Essex, 2001; Ingram et al., 2000).

Things to consider. Eastman and Swift (2002) noted that chat must be thoughtfully implemented and supported by the instructor. Many online instructors and/or researchers (e.g., Branon & Essex, 2001; Eastman & Swift, 2002; Kittleson, 2002) have stated that a protocol must be established for chatting. Instructor tasks include keeping the group focused, informing students of what is acceptable and effective participation (Berzenyi, 2000), and promoting interactivity among learners (Bannan- Ritland, 2002).

Instant Messaging (IM)

Instant messaging defined. Instant messaging (IM) is a synchronous communication method that uses Internet technology to send real-time text messages (Dunne, 2002). The user creates a list of individuals (the "buddy list") that he/she wishes to communicate with; messages can be sent to one person or to several as long as the person(s) is online (Riva, 2002; Tyson, n.d.). Although secure IM software exists (for a fee), most nonbusiness users tend to use the publicly accessible (free) IM clients. Most IM programs have chat, file-sharing, the ability to share images and sounds, and a talk feature (Tyson, n.d.).

Educational uses of instant messaging. The most common users of IM are college, high, and junior high students so there has not been much attention to use of IM in higher education (Cohn, 2002). Farmer (2003) surveyed college students and found that IM is strong and gaining on e-mail as their primary online communication tool; faculty members, however, have been slow to embrace this technology.

IM can be used for learner-instructor communication, collaboration on research projects, virtual conferences, remote guest speakers, class discussions, and prompt feedback (Cohn, 2002; Farmer, 2003; Fetterman, 2002; Tyson, n.d.). Farmer reported that incorporation of IM into online instruction can increase the social presence of distance students. Fetterman reported, however, that chat rooms might be better than IM for extended discussion.

Advantages of instant messaging. Farmer (2003) stated that for communication to be effective on the Internet, immediate and constant connectivity is essential. Benefits of IM include its ease of use and the ability to communicate in real time. Users can maintain control of their contact list, converse with more than one person at a time, and block messages from specific individuals (Dunne, 2002).

Disadvantages of instant messaging. There is a problem with interoperability when using most free IM clients (Tyson, n.d.). Farmer (2003) noted that major drawbacks include privacy and security concerns, although secure IM software addresses some of these issues. IM also has the potential to be a great "time waster."

Things to consider. Farmer (2003) characterized IM as the "faculty nightmare." Use of IM adds to the growing expectation of instructors being available at all times; it also adds more time to the faculty workload. Cohn (2002) noted that with the increased usage of communication tools like IM, faculty members are going to need the ability to simultaneously attend to several different activities.

Audio and Video Web-Based Conferencing (Audioconferencing and Videoconferencing)

Audio and video Web-based conferencing defined. Audioconferencing is a synchronous technology that allows verbal interaction among individuals or groups at a distance. Videoconferencing describes a system where multiple non-collocated participants communicate, see, and hear each other in real time, using a combination of technologies.

Educational uses of audio and video Web-based conferencing. Audioconferences are useful when verbal interaction between the educational participants is most important. Videoconferencing provides opportunities for higher level thinking via live face-to-face interaction with peers, tutors, or experts. Videoconferencing mitigates the disadvantages of learning at a distance through real-time interactive experiences, without regard to location. A partial list of activities includes practicing language speaking with native speakers, team teaching between locations, presenting student and teacher resources, communicating with mentors and subject matter experts, observing demonstrations in other schools, sharing experiences with students from other cultures, and enhancing learning at a distance (SBC, 2004).

Advantages of audio and video Web-based conferences. Software programs can be used in conjunction with the video and audio feeds to allow file exchange or collaborative work. If the instructor relies on conceptual comments and uses few or no graphics, audioconferences are a low cost alternative to a videoconference. Videoconferences most closely replicate the traditional, face-to-face classroom experience.

Disadvantages of audio and video Web-based conferences. Users without computer expertise may find setting up the systems and connecting for a conference challenging. Since both are synchronous systems, users must participate in real time. High-quality videoconferencing requires high-speed Internet connections, further limiting participation.

Things to consider. Students should be provided with detailed technical specifications and instructions well in advance of scheduled activities. A trial run eliminates many problems that may occur. Provisions should be made for recording the session so that students can review materials presented. Pre-instructional activities (such as directed readings or providing questions prior to the conference) will also help promote engagement.

CONCLUSION

All of the CMC tools (asynchronous and synchronous) discussed here have been proven or have the potential to increase interaction and enhance learning in the online environment. CMC tools themselves continue to evolve in terms of the features they include, and new tools may be developed. While the focus on student learning remains constant, online instructors will find that their instructional strategies must be flexible. Bender (2003) noted that it is critical for online instructors to develop a high level of comfort with technology to accompany subject matter expertise. Peirce (2003) summed up the rewards and challenges: "[O]nline professors can aim higher than merely teaching competent thinking. They can promote intellectual growth and encourage students to question favored approaches and methodologies that dominate our disciplines" (pp. 336-337).

REFERENCES

Anderson, K. (1999). Internet-based model of distance education. *Human Resource Development International, 2,* 259-272.

Angeli, C., Valanides, N., & Bonk, C. J. (2003). Communication in a Web-based conferencing system: The quality of computer-mediated interactions. *British Journal of Educational Technology, 34*(1), 31-43.

Bannan-Ritland, B. (2002). Computer-mediated communication, elearning, and interactivity: A review of the research. *The Quarterly Review of Distance Education, 3,* 161-179.

Bender, T. (2003). *Discussion-based online teaching to enhance student learning: Theory, practice and assessment.* Sterling, VA: Stylus.

Berzenyi, C. A. (2000). How to conduct a course-based computer chat room: Enabling a space for active learning. *Teaching English in the Two-Year College, 28*, 165-174.

Branon, R., & Essex, C. (2001). Synchronous and asynchronous communication tools in distance education. *TechTrends, 45*(1), 36, 42.

Burnett, C. (2003). Learning to chat: Tutor participation in synchronous online chat. *Teaching in Higher Education, 8*, 247-261.

Chen, D-T., & Hung, D. (2002). Personalised knowledge representations: The missing half of online discussions. *British Journal of Educational Technology, 33*, 279-290.

Cohn, E. R. (2002). *Instant messaging in higher education: A new faculty development challenge.* Retrieved January 28, 2004, from http://www.ipfw.edu/as/tohe/2002/Papers/cohn2.htm.

Dunne, D. (2002, October 16). *What is instant messaging?* Retrieved February 20, 2004, from http://www.darwinmag.com/learn/curve/column.html?ArticleID=151.

Eastman, J. K., & Swift, C. O. (2002). Enhancing collaborative learning: Discussion boards and chat rooms as project communication tools. *Business Communication Quarterly, 65*(3), 29-41.

Farmer, R. (2003). *Instant messaging–collaborative tool or educator's nightmare!* Retrieved February 20, 2004, from http://naWeb.unb.ca/proceedings/2003/PaperFarmer.html.

Farrior, E. S., & Gallagher, M. L. (2000). An evaluation of distance education. *Topics in Clinical Nutrition, 15*(4), 10-18.

Fetterman, D. M. (2002). Web surveys to digital movies: Technological tools of the trade. *Educational Researcher, 31*(6), 29-37.

Gonzales, C. L., & de Montes, L. S. (2001). Effective practices in distance education. *Computers in the Schools, 18*(2/3), 61-77.

Harrsch, M. (2003, July/August). RSS: The next killer app for education. *The Technology Source.* Retrieved February 15, 2004, from http://ts.mivu.org/default.asp?show=article&id=2010.

Hirumi, A. (2002). The design and sequencing of e-learning interactions: A grounded approach. *International Journal on E-Learning, 1*(1), 19-27.

Honeycutt, L. (2001). Comparing e-mail and synchronous conferencing in online peer response. *Written Communication, 18*(1), 26-60.

Hughes, C., & Hewson, L. (2001). Structuring communications to facilitate effective teaching and learning online. In C. D. Maddux & D. L. Johnson (Eds.), *The Web in higher education: Assessing the impact and fulfilling the potential* (pp. 147-158). New York: Haworth Press.

Hyman, A. (2003). Twenty years of ListServ as an academic tool. *Internet and Higher Education, 6*, 17-24.

Im, Y., & Lee, O. (2003/2004). Pedagogical implications of online discussion for preservice teacher training. *Journal of Research on Technology in Education, 36*, 155-170.

Ingram, A. L., Hathorn, L. G., & Evans. A. (2000). Beyond chat on the Internet. *Computers and Education, 35*, 21-35.

Johnson, M. M., & Huff, M. T. (2000). Students' use of computer-mediated communication in a distance education course. *Research on Social Work Practice, 10*, 519-532.

Jung, I., Choi, S., Lim, C., & Leem, J. (2002). Effects of different types of interaction on learning achievement, satisfaction and participation in Web-based instruction. *Innovations in Education and Teaching International, 39*, 153-162.

Kirk, R. (2000). A study of the use of a private chat room to increase reflective thinking in pre-service teachers. *College Student Journal, 34*, 115+. Retrieved February 14, 2004, from Academic Search Premier database.

Kittleson, M. J. (2002). Chat room protocol. *American Journal of Health Behavior, 26*, 229-230.

Knowlton, D. S. (2003). Evaluating college students' efforts in asynchronous discussion: A systematic process. *The Quarterly Review of Distance Education, 4*(1), 31-41.

Lapadat, J. C. (2002). Written interaction: A key component in online learning. *Journal of Computer-Mediated Communication, 7*(4). Retrieved October 13, 2003, from http://www.ascusc.org/jcmc/vol7/issue4/lapadat.html.

McKeage, K. (2001). Office hours as you like them. *College Teaching, 49*(1), 32+. Retrieved September 10, 2003, from Academic Search Premier database.

Mitchell, D. (2004). *Thoughts about Weblogs in education.* Retrieved February 15, 2004, from http://www.teachnology.org/stories/storyReader$150.

Moore, M. G. (1989). Editorial: Three types of interaction. *The American Journal of Distance Education, 3*(2), 1-6.

Murphy, G. (2003). *RSS–The downside.* Retrieved February 15, 2004, from http://www.criticalmethods.org/collab/v.mv?d=1_1.

Ng, K. (2001). Using e-mail to foster collaboration in distance education. *Open Learning, 16*, 191-200.

Peirce, W. (2003). Strategies for teaching thinking and promoting intellectual development in online classes. In S. Reisman (Ed.), *Electronic learning communities: Issues and practices* (pp. 301-347). Greenwich, CT: Information Age Publishing.

Richardson, W. (2003). *FAQ–How do Weblogs impact learning?* Retrieved February 8, 2004, from http://www.Weblogg-ed.com/stories/storyReader$414.

Richardson, W. (2004). Blogging and RSS–The "what's it?" and "how to" of powerful new tools for Web educators. *Multimedia & Internet@Schools, 11*(1), 10-13. Retrieved February 15, 2004, from http://www.infotoday.com/MMSchools/jan04/richardson.shtml.

Riva, G. (2002). The sociocognitive psychology of computer-mediated communication: The present and future of technology-based interactions. *Cyberpsychology and Behavior, 5*, 581-598.

SBC Knowledge Network Explorer. (2004). *Videoconferencing for learning.* Retrieved February 15, 2004, from http://www.kn.pacbell.com/wired/vidconf/.

Tiene, D. (2000). Online discussions: A survey of advantages and disadvantages compared to face-to-face discussions. *Journal of Educational Multimedia and Hypermedia, 9*, 371-384.

Tiene, D. (2002). Digital multimedia and distance education: Can they effectively be combined? *T.H.E. Journal, 29*(9), 18+. Retrieved September 10, 2003, from Academic Search Premier database.

Tyson, J. (n.d.). *How instant messaging works.* Retrieved February 20, 2004, from http://www.howstuffworks.com/instant-messaging.htm.

Vonderwell, S. (2003). An examination of asynchronous communication experiences and perspectives of students in an online course: A case study. *Internet and Higher Education, 6,* 77-90.

Wang, A. Y., & Newlin, M. H. (2001). Online lectures: Benefits for the virtual classroom. *T.H.E. Journal, 29*(1), 17+. Retrieved February 14, 2004, from Academic Search Premier database.

Lih-Ching Chen Wang
William Beasley

Type II Technology Applications in Teacher Education: Using Instant Messenger to Implement Structured Online Class Discussions

SUMMARY. The use of the Instant Messenger (IM) environment to carry out structured online class discussions in graduate teacher education courses is described. Properties of IM are delineated, and specific procedures in using IM as a vehicle for class discussions are discussed. Attributes of Type II technology applications are addressed directly, and the characteristics of these class activities that correspond with such attributes are discussed in detail. In closing, the authors draw a clear distinction between casual IM use in a class setting and planned,

LIH-CHING CHEN WANG is Associate Professor of Educational Technology, Department of Curriculum and Foundations, College of Education and Human Services, Cleveland State University, Cleveland, OH 44115-2214 (E-mail: l.c.wang@csuohio.edu).

WILLIAM BEASLEY is Associate Professor of Educational Technology, Department of Curriculum and Foundations, College of Education and Human Services, and Director of the University Center for Teaching & Learning, Cleveland State University, Cleveland, OH 44115-2214 (E-mail: w.beasley@csuohio.edu).

[Haworth co-indexing entry note]: "Type II Technology Applications in Teacher Education: Using Instant Messenger to Implement Structured Online Class Discussions." Wang, Lih-Ching Chen, and William Beasley. Co-published simultaneously in *Computers in the Schools* (The Haworth Press, Inc.) Vol. 22, No. 1/2, 2005, pp. 71-84; and: *Internet Applications of Type II Uses of Technology in Education* (ed: Cleborne D. Maddux, and D. LaMont Johnson) The Haworth Press, Inc., 2005, pp. 71-84. Single or multiple copies of this article are available for a fee from The Haworth Document Delivery Service [1-800-HAWORTH, 9:00 a.m. - 5:00 p.m. (EST). E-mail address: docdelivery@haworthpress.com].

Available online at http://www.haworthpress.com/web/CITS
© 2005 by The Haworth Press, Inc. All rights reserved.
Digital Object Identifier: 10.1300/J025v22n01_07

structured implementation of IM as an example of a Type II technology application. *[Article copies available for a fee from The Haworth Document Delivery Service: 1-800-HAWORTH. E-mail address: <docdelivery@haworthpress. com> Website: <http://www.HaworthPress.com> © 2005 by The Haworth Press, Inc. All rights reserved.]*

KEYWORDS. Instant Messenger, IM, America Online Instant Messenger, AIM, Type II technology applications, technology integration, online class discussion, synchronous communication, computer-mediated communication, CMC

Much work in the field of computer-mediated communications (CMC) has focused on the use of tools such as computer conferencing in education. Brand (1988, p. xiii) noted significantly that "communications media are so fundamental to a society that when their structure changes, everything is affected." Eastmond (1994) proposed a systematic model for factors involved in using computer conferencing in adult distance education classes. Harasim, Hiltz, Teles, and Turoff (1995) articulated a variety of specific asynchronous online learning activities and made a strong case for these activities as fostering interaction both among students and between students and instructors.

Lauzon (1992) noted the challenge faced by distance educators to move students from being recipients of knowledge to being active participants–clearly a constructivist perspective. Bullen (1998) provided a thoughtful case study of a university-level course delivered by computer conferencing, and closely examined the effect of the technology on class participation and critical thinking. Meanwhile, Eastmond and Granger (1998) used computer conferencing, referred to as Type II technology, to enhance instructional communication.

Bullen's computer conferencing was implicitly an *asynchronous* activity, and in fact, much of Bullen's analysis was focused on that attribute of the learning experience. This article reports on a similar but significantly different technology–that of instant messaging (IM). IM is implicitly *synchronous*, but otherwise involves students gathering online in a shared text-only environment for class activities very much as does an asynchronous threaded discussion.

WHAT IS INSTANT MESSENGER (IM)?

IM software allows conversations between two or more individuals online in real time. It is much like Citizens Band radio in that it provides a "shared space" in which semi-public communication can occur, but IM takes place via keyboards rather than microphones, and on the Internet rather than the radio airwaves. Most IM programs are free to be downloaded from the Internet; two of the best known IM programs in recent times are America Online Instant Messenger (AIM) and Microsoft Network (MSN) Messenger.

The popularity (and feature set) of these programs has increased dramatically, and with these changes has come an increasing willingness on the part of educators to use IM to enhance teaching and learning activities. One of the authors has been using AIM software both for student advising and for structured class learning activities for five semesters at the time of this writing, and has found the process to be both complex and valuable.

The purpose of this paper is not to report formal data analysis, but to report the experiences observed directly by the instructor in the process of using IM for instructional purposes, and to provide more information about one potential instructional Type II technique that may be of value to other teachers and students.

METHODOLOGY

Context and Design

The activities described were conducted with graduate students from an educational technology program in teacher education at a Midwestern urban state university. They were mostly in-service K-12 educators.

The class format was Internet-based with the exception of two face-to-face class meetings. One was an initial introductory class occurring at the beginning of the semester, and the other was used for final project presentations and held at the end of the semester. All other class activities took place online. The class met once a week for four hours in the online environment, including one hour of formal online chapter discussion entirely in the IM environment; the instructor deliberately limited formal discussion to one hour at a time to avoid student fatigue and maximize efficiency. The other three hours of class time included activities such as student use of the class file server for class activities, online peer communications or collaborations on class-related activities, and use of the instructor's online office hours. See Wang and Beasley (in press) for more details on the integration of IM into online office hours.

Procedure

Skills. At the initial class session, all students were taught how to download and install the (free) AIM software. Students were taught a set of basic AIM skills, including those involved in carrying out a discussion and saving the contents of the discussion to disk. They were also taught to upload and download files using a class file server, in order to ensure their ability to post and read materials provided by any member of the class. Students learned that during the rest of the semester they would be required to participate in a series of class discussions, centering around assigned topics drawn from major chapters in the required class text. The discussions would take place entirely within the IM environment and would occur on a schedule to be provided by the instructor. Students were informed that their contributions should be chapter related and that the frequency of each student's participation in the discussion would be noted by the instructor.

To encourage students to quickly master the IM environment, the instructor actively promoted student use of IM for contacts between student and instructor as well as for contacts among classmates outside of class. During the second week, student use of IM consisted entirely of this type of contact, and students were able to consult actively with their classmates as well as with the instructor regarding any problems with using the IM software; they were also encouraged to use IM to interact with the classmate who was scheduled to lead the first discussion. After the second week, the main focus shifted to the use of IM for structured class discussions. At this time the "screen names" (aliases) employed by AIM were made available as a list to all class members, enabling any student to initiate contact with the entire class using a single mouse click within the IM environment.

Discussion leaders. The requirements for fulfilling the leader role were substantial and thoroughly documented in materials provided to the students. The instructor played an active role in choosing the leaders of the first discussions, in an effort to ensure a successful first encounter, though initial leaders were chosen with the full consent of the individual students involved.

Each leader was required to prepare a presentation PowerPoint file that included preparatory materials for the topic he/she chose to lead in the discussion. Required contents included: (a) summary of the chapter, (b) feedback or critique on the chapter, (c) examples of situations drawn from the chapter that he/she could implement into a student teaching or learning setting, and (d) at least three critical inquiry questions drawn from the chapter. The file itself, along with a word-processed document addressing chapter details, was submitted by the discussion leader to the common folder in the class file server three days before the discussion.

The leader was required to log in to the discussion at least 15 minutes prior to the starting time to prepare for the discussion activities and/or to chat informally with any classmates online. At the appointed time, the leader was to invite classmates into the scheduled group chat. During the discussion, it was the student leader's role to initiate the discussion by posting discussion questions drawn from the previously distributed PowerPoint and word processor files. His/her task was then to be the teacher of the moment, to answer questions raised by the participants and to stimulate or facilitate the discussion process.

It should be noted that the instructor did not "disappear" from the discussion. Throughout the online discussion period, the instructor also participated with the students. The instructor took the online attendance, invited late-comers into the group chat, observed the discussion, answered individual inquiries, asked questions, solved problems, and facilitated the discussion as needed. In many ways, the course instructor served as a teaching assistant to the leader during these discussion periods. At the end of discussion, the leader was required to save the discussion transcript and distribute to the class.

Individual participants. After each student leader posted the chapter files in the common folder of the class file server, but before the discussion session, all other students were asked to access these files and organize their thoughts in preparation for the discussion. They were encouraged to post and share their own chapter commentary with the rest of the class, using the class file server, and awarded bonus points for doing so.

All students were required to log in to the discussion area 10 minutes prior to the scheduled discussion time. After the discussion was over (but prior to the next scheduled discussion), each participant was to electronically organize personal reflections, feedback, and notes on the chapter and then post these to his/her own personal electronic portfolio (*e*Portfolio) on the class file server for evaluation. Online attendance, quantity and quality of a student's online interaction, and *e*Portfolio constituted 10% of a student's final grade.

Outcomes. The introductory procedures worked well. All class members were able to log on at the appointed time for the first discussion, and all were able to enter the designated AIM discussion group. The assigned discussion leaders followed all guidelines provided by the instructor, showing up online 15 minutes before the discussion time, and taking care to "invite" those participants who were wandering around "outside" into the designated discussion group. The online discussions proceeded as expected, with facilitation primarily from the assigned student leader, and the instructor in the background to observe and assist.

An interesting development was the fact that less-knowledgeable students in the group continued to expand and enhance the complexity of their IM skills throughout the semester, through individual interaction with their more competent classmates as well as with the instructor. While the introductory lessons and practice in the use of AIM were sufficient to bring all students to an adequate level of competency, it quickly became evident that there was a wide range of skills in the group, and those with less mastery aspired to emulate their more sophisticated classmates.

IM-BASED LEARNING ACTIVITIES AS TYPE II TECHNOLOGY APPLICATIONS

Maddux, Johnson, and Willis (2001) have suggested that technology applications in education can by categorized into two types. Type I applications focus on providing more convenient or efficient ways of carrying out traditional learning or teaching activities, and tend to involve a teacher-centered focus. Type II applications are more student-centered, and focus on providing ways to teach or learn that are not possible (or practical) in the absence of technology. In explaining their categorization, they specified five characteristics of Type II applications. As implemented in the instructor's own experience, IM embodies these five characteristics in the following ways (summarized in Table 1).

Since it is abundantly clear that simply using IM in a classroom setting does not automatically create a Type II technology use scenario, we will examine in greater detail the ways in which this particular class implementation of IM embodies these five characteristics, focusing on one example through which the appropriate use of IM may legitimately be described as "Type II."

Type II Activities Stimulate Relatively Active Intellectual Involvement

Well-orchestrated classroom discussions have long been chosen as a learning activity in order to stimulate active intellectual involvement on the part of students, and the techniques of assigning students to discus-

TABLE 1. Summary of IM-Based Learning Activities as Type II Technology Applications

Characteristics (Type II activities)	IM properties (as implemented)
1. Stimulate relatively active intellectual involvement	• Student was assigned the responsibility for leading and moderating chapter discussions (student as an active instructor) • All students were required to actively participate in each discussion session
2. Place the learner rather the developer (e.g., teacher) in charge of the learning environment	• Student and instructor have almost equal levels of control over IM environment, although instructor can still control access to discussions • Students retain full ability for communication among one another "on the side" without instructor's knowledge or control
3. Provide the learner with control over the interaction between the user and the machine, with extensive repertoire of acceptable user input	• Students have control over individual forms of expression within IM software (e.g., colors, styles, emoticons) • Student and instructor both have simultaneous access to other programs (e.g., PowerPoint, word processor, Web browser, spreadsheet) with ability to move among programs and discussion during live discussion
4. Have the accomplishment of creative tasks as their goal	• Collaborative discussion (an intrinsically creative action) led by students is explicit goal of IM activities in this situation • Archived discussion contents in text form are automated, readily distributable and extensible
5. Require many hours to discover full potential of the software or software-based activity	• Full repertoire of IM-based discussion techniques (e.g., interweaving other resources live, employing private side conversations) takes significant time to master

sion leadership roles and requiring structured discussion preparation are time-honored procedures within traditional instruction. In our situation, IM software was used to implement these procedures in a relatively novel environment–one in which the class participants were not in physical proximity to one another.

Every student in the class was assigned to lead a formally scheduled chapter discussion within the IM environment. This role placed three major demands on an individual student: the first was a substantial level of formal preparation regarding the chapter contents; the second was to serve as the discussion leader and facilitator throughout the hour of the online session; the third was to distribute to all class members a transcript of the discussion after its conclusion. These individuals were in effect "teacher for a day." To carry out these demands required an intensively active involvement on the part of the discussion leader, and as has been noted, every student fulfilled the role of discussion leader at some point during the semester.

While individual participants were subject to fewer demands, all students were required to actively participate in all discussions. As noted, attendance was required, quality of participation was monitored, and all students were to post their reflections and thoughts about each discussion. The fact that all discussion content was automatically archived made it easy to determine quality and quantity of participation for each class member.

While the most active intellectual involvement in each discussion was that of the assigned discussion leader, the combination of the IM environment with structured participation requirements clearly stimulated relatively active intellectual involvement on the part of other individuals in the class.

Type II Activities Place the Learner Rather Than the Developer (e.g., Teacher) in Charge of the Learning Environment

In many ways the IM environment is highly egalitarian. It was originally developed not for instructional purposes, but for the use of individuals who wished to communicate synchronously with friends and colleagues. Its structure is built around an equal level of "power" to all participants. The only special capability available is the power of an individual who originates an online discussion to control the entry of others into that discussion area. In the context of this class, the teacher was the one figure who originated the class discussions, and thus retained that power. As it happens, any student could theoretically have set up another discussion, over which he or she would have retained control in the same sense. The teacher in this context is "first among equals" with regard to power over the discussion environment.

As the class discussions were simply one group conversation taking place in the IM environment, students were able not only to participate in other online discussions at the same time, but also to enter into private "side conversations"–either with other class members, or with other individuals present in the IM environment. Obviously, this is not entirely positive, but it *is* a clear indication that students retain a high degree of control over the learning environment. The instructor has the same capability, and it was often used for private conversations between instructor and student "on the fly"–a sort of ad hoc online office hours in mid-discussion.

It is clear that in this IM-based learning environment, students and instructor shared an almost equal level of control over the learning environment, freeing students from the traditionally passive role of information recipient and shifting the instructor into a facilitator role.

Type II Activities Provide the Learner with Control Over the Interaction Between the User and the Machine, with Extensive Repertoire of Acceptable User Input

This third characteristic focuses on what happens *within* the context of IM-based learning. Formatted text, essentially limited to the characters available on a computer keyboard plus a limited selection of standardized icons (e.g., "smiley faces"), is the primary medium of IM communication. While this sounds limited, in skilled hands a surprising variety of techniques is possible, ranging from the use of emoticons to convey body language or emotional content (e.g., ";-)" to indicate a winking) to the use of URLs within IM to allow immediate links to Web pages containing images or auditory content that can be incorporated into an IM discussion. Each participant in IM retains control over these components, as well as other related variables such as text color, size, font, and style. In this respect, control over form of expression within IM is absolutely equal between student and instructor; each has the same tool set.

Since the IM client is simply one program among many on a computer's desktop, each participant retains access to other software on his/her computer while the IM discussion is in progress. One may move freely among the programs, and use information from these other programs to inform the discussion. For example, if numbers and calculations enter the discussion, any participant can fire up Excel on the side and check a set of figures, bringing the results back into the IM environment via copy and paste. Another common example: in mid-discussion, a participant may launch a Web browser and conduct a quick Google search for relevant Web pages. This information is promptly pasted into the IM environment, and all other participants are enabled to link immediately to the relevant source in mid-discussion. These capabilities were actively used by the students, who also regularly used PowerPoint and Word during IM discussions to refer back to information provided by each student discussion leader in advance of each discussion.

It is clear that through activities such as using different modes of expression within the IM environment and navigating among varied programs simultaneously during IM discussions, the IM-based environment can provide learners with control over the interaction between the user and the machine, allowing for an extensive repertoire of acceptable student input.

Type II Activities Have the Accomplishment of Creative Tasks as Their Goal

A fundamental concept underlying Type II activities is that they are intended for the accomplishment of a creative task. A collaborative discussion, properly conducted, is an intrinsically creative task. As implemented in this particular case, each discussion was led by a student who was required to prepare intensively for the event, creating and distributing in advance to classmates materials dealing with a particular set of concepts. This preparation was itself a creative activity, but the real point was the discussion itself as it evolved online in the IM environment. Such a discussion incorporates unique and highly individualized perspectives on the topic(s) at hand from the viewpoint of each student in the class, resulting in a tapestry of ideas that is different each time such a discussion occurs.

This would be true of a high-quality class discussion, even if technology were not involved–but the incorporation of the IM environment brings an additional set of properties to the process that strengthens and enhances student interaction with the content of the discussion. When such a discussion takes place using IM, the entire discussion in text form is automatically archived, readily distributable and extensible, forming the basis for further elaboration at a later time. This concurs with Ligorio's (2001) statement that providing chances for re-reading and reflecting on what has been written facilitates the immediacy of the synchronous online chatting process. The result is that an IM-based discussion–as a creative act–can continue over an extended period of time following the original discussion, producing a continuously expanding and evolving creative dialogue to address the original discussion topics.

Type II Activities Require Many Hours to Discover Full Potential of the Software or Software-Based Activity

Using this characteristic to describe IM-based discussions is a slight departure from Maddux, Johnson, and Willis's (2001) use of "Type II" to characterize specific pieces of software (e.g., the "Sim" series). As a piece of software, IM is not a complex program that requires long hours of discovery–but it does in fact require many hours of use for an instructor (and students) to discover all the ways in which a rich, deep, multi-faceted, and technologically interwoven group discussion can take place in an IM environment. The skills necessary for a student to simply participate in an IM discussion are easily mastered, but experience shows that the IM environment has the potential for surprising depth through the incorporation of specific techniques that extend the range of the discussion to incorporate far more than simply verbal statements from individuals. Two techniques that were used heavily during these discussions were individual side conversations (both between instructor and student, and between pairs of students) and the incorporation into the discussion of information gleaned from the use of other programs running simultaneously on a student's or instructor's computer (e.g., URLs from concurrent Web searches). Clearly, full mastery of all the discussion-related potential of the IM environment requires considerable time and practice to master.

LIMITATIONS

In both traditional and IM-based discussions, there are certain commonalities. In both cases, the instructor has an opportunity to prepare students for the discussion ahead of time, and to establish expectations and parameters intended to guide the discussion. In both cases, all students have the potential to participate in the discussion, albeit via two different media (voice or keyboard). In both cases, the instructor can check attendance for all students participating. In both cases, the instructor can be present and can respond directly to student questions either privately or in such a way that the entire group can be aware of the question and answer.

The IM environment itself has certain limitations that are not present in a more traditional class setting, and it is important to acknowledge those; many are due to IM's reliance on text-based communication. Although most students type more slowly than they speak, IM requires individual expression to take place via the keyboard–and although some students comprehend (and compose) the spoken word more readily than the written word, all IM communication uses the written word. Non-verbal cues (e.g., body language, tone of voice) are largely absent in the IM environment, and when present are done using artificial means such as emoticons, which do not come naturally to new users. Unlike a traditional discussion in which protocol dictates that only one person speak at a time, IM discussions allow many simultaneous "speakers"–which can result in the phenomenon of "flooding," in which one's screen fills rapidly with too much content in too many threads from too many participants and rapidly overwhelms novice users. IM software accepts only a limited number of text characters in each posting, resulting in a need to break long statements into multiple postings, which may become separated by content from other participants and thus rendered less intact conceptually. All in all, the attributes of an entirely text-based exchange of ideas are sufficiently unfamiliar to some students to serve as a discouraging factor, potentially reducing their participation.

Two other limitations of the IM environment are due to its highly technological roots. It relies heavily on a reliable Internet connection for all participants, and it requires an instructor or moderator able to "think fast" and act on his/her feet due both to simultaneity of student response and to a need to troubleshoot occasional software or equipment difficulties in mid-discussion.

CONCLUSION

This paper is rooted in the concept of Type II technology applications; as Maddux, Johnson, and Willis (2001) have noted, such activities go beyond simply automating traditional learning applications and enable learning activities that would not be feasible without technology. Since this paper is also focused on class discussion, and since class discussion can be a very traditional learning application, the burden placed upon this paper is that of demonstrating that, when correctly planned and implemented, the use of an IM environment for class discussion does in fact go beyond simply automating what would take place in a traditional classroom, even though it takes place synchronously and covers much of the same course content.

Moving class discussions into IM causes the discussion to become logically independent of the participants' physical location. While useful and perhaps even essential in the case of distance education courses, it is doubtful whether this property alone is sufficient to warrant a Type II descriptor. Simply holding class discussions using IM does not in and of itself constitute a Type II technology application; it is the *way* in which class discussions are held using IM that can make the difference.

This paper has documented the instructor's methodology for moving IM-based classroom discussions solidly into the Type II arena. First, the instructor required all students to take on the role of discussion leader, and provided structure for the actions required of the discussion leader in advance preparation and discussion moderation. The instructor also made quantity and quality of participation in the online discussions part of the class evaluation scheme, and followed up by taking roll online and monitoring student participation. These actions stimulated relatively active intellectual involvement.

Second, the instructor chose to use the IM environment (as opposed to other possible text-based synchronous environments, such as IRC or WebCT chat), which preserved a high level of individual student control over the environment in which the discussions took place. This placed the learner in charge of the learning environment, including providing students with the ability to carry on multiple parallel communications or activities during the class discussion.

Third, rather than imposing a limited and formal structure for communication within the discussion, the instructor embraced the variety available within IM, welcoming student use of colors, styles, and icons and actively encouraging students to make use of multiple programs during class discussions in order to provide deeper and more complex fuel for the conversation at hand. This gave learners a large degree of control over the interaction within the IM environment and encouraged a maximum richness of content.

Fourth, the instructor built student-led chapter discussions into the structure of the course, including the active distribution of archived discussions to all participants and an individual *e*Portfolio area where students posted their reflections, observations, and questions about discussions after the fact. The resulting discussions and associated communications came to constitute an extended, group-authored creative task and were one of the main goals of the class.

Finally, the instructor chose to forego a strictly limited tool or implementation in favor of a relatively complex tool that may be quickly and easily used for simple activities but that requires many hours to master, and to directly encourage students to pursue the deepest and most complex ways of using the chosen tool–thus fulfilling the final Type II characteristic of requiring many hours to discover the full potential of the activity.

In summary, the type of IM-based class discussions and their attendant online interactions described herein fully embody the characteristics of Type II technology applications, and as such provide a powerful learning tool that can be used with traditional classes but has particular application to distance learning courses. It is the experience of the instructor that these activities empower students to use technology to create their own learning environments filled with enthusiasm and self-motivation–one of the best settings for teaching and learning success.

REFERENCES

Brand, S. (1988). *The media lab: Inventing the future at MIT*. New York: Penguin Books.

Bullen, M. (1998). Participation and critical thinking in online university distance education. *Journal of Distance Education, 13*(2) [Online]. Retrieved February 20, 2004, from http://cade.athabascau.ca/vol13.2/bullen.html

Eastmond, D. (1994). Adult distance study through computer conferencing. *Distance Education, 15*(1), 128-152.

Eastmond, D., & Granger, D. (1998). Using Type II computer network technology to reach distance students. *Distance Education Report, 2*(3), 1-3 & 8.

Harasim, L., Hiltz, S., Teles, L., & Turoff, M. (1995). *Learning networks: A field guide to teaching and learning online*. Cambridge, MA: MIT Press.

Lauzon, A. C. (1992). Integrating computer-based instruction with computer conferencing: An evaluation of a model for designing online education. *American Journal of Distance Education, 6*(2), 32-46.

Ligorio, M. B. (2001). Integrating communication formats: Synchronous versus asynchronous and text-based versus visual. *Computers & Education, 37*(2), 103-125.

Maddux, C., Johnson, D., & Willis, J. (2001). *Educational computing: Learning with tomorrow's technology* (3rd ed.). Boston: Allyn & Bacon.

Wang, L. C., & Beasley, W. (in press). Integrating Instant Messenger into online office hours to enhance synchronous online interaction in teacher education. *International Journal of Instructional Media, 33*(3).

Laurel Smith Stvan

Inferring New Vocabulary Using Online Texts

SUMMARY. Through small-scale sampling of relevant specialized texts to craft hands-on inferential vocabulary tasks, both students and teachers can benefit from corpus linguistic information. By discovering ways to collect and access real data, second-language teachers can create topic-specific corpora and use software to sort and highlight the data to create more rich and revealing classroom materials for improving vocabulary learning. This student-centered, data-driven learning can be easily adapted for different levels of reading students. Free or purchased software, as well as features of existing programs, can be put to use to access online texts. *[Article copies available for a fee from The Haworth Document Delivery Service: 1-800-HAWORTH. E-mail address: <docdelivery@haworthpress.com> Website: <http://www.HaworthPress.com> © 2005 by The Haworth Press, Inc. All rights reserved.]*

KEYWORDS. Vocabulary, second-language acquisition, online texts, corpus linguistics, reading, context, concordancing

LAUREL SMITH STVAN is Assistant Professor, Department of Linguistics and TESOL, The University of Texas at Arlington, Arlington, TX 76019-0559 (E-mail: stvan@uta.edu).

[Haworth co-indexing entry note]: "Inferring New Vocabulary Using Online Texts." Stvan, Laurel Smith. Co-published simultaneously in *Computers in the Schools* (The Haworth Press, Inc.) Vol. 22, No. 1/2, 2005, pp. 85-96; and: *Internet Applications of Type II Uses of Technology in Education* (ed: Cleborne D. Maddux, and D. LaMont Johnson) The Haworth Press, Inc., 2005, pp. 85-96. Single or multiple copies of this article are available for a fee from The Haworth Document Delivery Service [1-800-HAWORTH, 9:00 a.m. - 5:00 p.m. (EST). E-mail address: docdelivery@haworthpress.com].

Available online at http://www.haworthpress.com/web/CITS
© 2005 by The Haworth Press, Inc. All rights reserved.
Digital Object Identifier: 10.1300/J025v22n01_08

One area that has greatly benefited from the use of new technology is language learning. Better explanations of language use have come about as scholars have been able to access and examine larger and larger samples of language, a task made easier by the increased speed and storage abilities of computers. Many dictionaries, for example, have improved their entries over the years by citing from collections of naturally occurring data rather than made-up examples. While reference works based on such a body or "corpus" of attested data date back as far as the first *Oxford English Dictionary* publication in 1884, recent works that rely on collections of computerized texts for the data, such as the *Collins COBUILD English Language Dictionary* (Sinclair, 1987) and the *Longman Grammar of Spoken and Written English* (Biber, Johansson, Leech, Conrad, & Finegan, 1999), have now set the standard.

Beyond verifying actual usage, much work in linguistic analysis has been clarified by data from real (often genre-focused) data. But without being trained in software that will concordance a text–that is, sort and highlight instances of the item in question–and without purchasing copies of large corpus collections, how can language teachers find a way to access the insights derived from corpora to enhance the tasks that language learners use in the classroom? By doing small-scale sampling of relevant specialized texts to craft hands-on inferential vocabulary tasks, both students and teachers can benefit from corpus linguistic information. In discovering ways to collect and access real data, they can create topic-specific corpora and then sample their data to create more rich and revealing classroom materials.

Maddux, Johnson, and Willis (2001) present definitions of contrasting types of technology uses in which they separate those uses that merely speed up or put a clean face on tasks that are already going on in teaching, from those that allow a new exploration of ideas. These second uses are the Type II technologies, those that allow students and teachers to use inductive reasoning, data manipulation, and individual encounters with material in new ways. Similarly, Warschauer (1996, 1998) details levels of technology use in language classrooms, sorting out those that are purely instrumental from those more critical approaches that can "bring about new power relations in a classroom or community" (1998, p. 759). One type of language learning task that is both student centered and data driven is determining vocabulary usage based on multiple, real-life examples. Allowing students to infer meaning and usage patterns, from collections of real language use is a prime Type II use of technology. And today, concordancing software and improved collections of text corpora make it easier to access relevant materials for each set of learners.

COMPUTERIZED TEXT CORPORA

Early work in compiling a language corpus was aimed at gathering large samples that represented a whole language. The one million word Brown Corpus gathered by Francis and Kucera (1967), for example, was a general language corpus made of American English texts excerpted from documents, journalism, and fiction published in 1961. As each corpus compiled since then has gotten bigger, researchers' ability to use it to more accurately describe the general language has improved as well. However, many teachers find that, in addition to general language vocabulary, their students need to become familiar with the language of a specialized subject or domain. For work, for travel, or for graduate studies, they need to read and master representative materials from a new genre. Thus, recent works like Bowker and Pearson (2002) and Ghadessy, Henry, and Roseberry (2001) focus on the insights to be gleaned from small, specialized text corpora.

Incorporating authentic language is not a new concept in communicative second-language teaching. Bringing in examples of real-life texts such as menus, cookbooks, appliance manuals, and job applications has been found to be a way to expose learners to the variety of text types that they may encounter in using a new language. The idea of collecting language samples of the type most useful to their students, therefore, is not out of line with many language teachers' training.

In discussions of ways to gather language examples, the World Wide Web is often put forward as a source of naturally occurring data. In many ways it is the ultimate free and ever-growing corpus. But the Web is not without its downsides. It contains a mix of native and non-native speaker utterances, a mix of edited and unedited sources, a mix of spoken, written, and multi-genre material, and is a repository of language from many different eras. In other words, the material to be found on the Web is often too uncontrolled to rely on for usage samples. Thus, especially for beginning students, the Web can offer poor data from which to draw conclusions.

For first-language learners, Miller and Gildea (1987) discuss the difficulties of acquiring word meanings through reading traditional printed texts. In an argument pre-dating the Web, they suggest a need for a method with more contextual options available at precisely the spot where the words in question appear, rather than forcing a reader's eyes to leave his current sentence while he goes to look up the word in another book. Furthermore, when readers do move to a dictionary, they are forced to guess from multiple senses in a dictionary entry which one best matches their word's original context, by which time that context may now be gone from short-term memory. Second-language readers face the same problems, of course, with the added difficulty of having had even less exposure to the new term to help them to puzzle out the correct sense.

Hyperlinking abilities across computer networks, as well as the ability to simultaneously access multiple applications, as is now found in most operating systems (OS), have eliminated some of the problems of a reader moving from book to book. That is, the modern reader does much of his or her reading and reference work in front of a single screen, with the ability to immediately click back and forth to seek further information.

LANGUAGE TASKS THAT CAN EXPLOIT THESE TECHNOLOGIES

Thus, OS software is rapidly improving to make it easier for readers to deal with new words. How can application software supplement this? Two kinds of linguistic software come into play: (a) collections of text corpora, and (b) concordancing and indexing tools to analyze them. Electronic corpus material is now being used in many ways to enhance language teaching, as can be seen, for example, in the special 2001 issue of *Language Learning and Technology* (volume 5, number 3) focusing on using corpora in language instruction. The improvement of grammars and dictionaries, mentioned earlier, has been one such outcome. Another focus is for second-language teachers to collect examples of writing produced by non-native speakers of a language in order to find error patterns in the use and acquisition of second-language grammar (e.g., Granger, 1998). These usages are then contrasted with a corpus of native speaker data that serves as the target usage. Most corpora, however, including those proposed in this article, focus only on collecting the language produced by native speakers.

Another application of text corpora is in translation; here work often relies on "parallel corpora"–two translations of the same material. With these, students examine aligned segments of the texts to observe contrasting constructions. (Special software–such as Multiconcord, created by David Woolls at University of Birmingham, and the WinAlign features of Trados Freelance–is available to align translated texts.)

Finally, in writing instruction, corpora are especially useful as representative genres or styles that can be accessed as models for writers, in both discourse layout (such as contrastive rhetoric) and academic or other specialized vocabulary. For details on using corpora in writing instruction, see work by Chris Tribble (1997, 2001a, 2001b among others).

As can be seen from the examples above, much language teaching could benefit from Type II technology uses such as accessing computerized corpora. In this paper, however, the focus will be on a skill that plays a crucial role in reading classes, but also in many other areas of language study: vocabulary acquisition. Concordances have been produced for centuries, as every word of a particular body of work–say the Bible, the Koran, or the complete works of Shakespeare–was meticulously itemized by hand to show the distribution of each word in the oeuvre. For language students, using a concordance allows a chance to learn vocabulary nuances from context. That is, students act as their own lexicographers, discerning senses from a set of real uses in context. This is what Johns calls "data-driven learning" (Hadley, 2002; Johns, 1994). Research has shown that readers make use of different techniques in engaging with text. They may do intensive reading, which involves carefully working through a text word for word; extensive reading, where readers move more quickly, as in pleasure reading; skimming, in which they attempt to gather the gist of a text; and scanning, in which they hunt for a particular piece or type of information. A computerized concordance program itself works at the scanning stage, moving quickly through a text of any size, and collecting each occurrence of the word in question into a list in which each line shows one sentence using that word, with the key word highlighted. With this list in hand, a student has the data needed to proceed with his/her observations and to try out inductive strategies in order to sort out the senses and uses of the word. (While it seems intuitively useful for students to be able to pull together examples via concordancing, the assumptions that such concordance-based vocabulary learning is, in fact, effective is explicitly tested and verified in Cobb [2004] in a study using a group of first year Arabic-speaking college students who were learning English. He found that learners consistently retained vocabulary knowledge at higher rates when they gathered the meanings by means of multiple-context examples–as offered by concordance software–than they did by using other methods of mastering new words.)

While students have the goal of reaching conclusions based on contrasting output from a concordance program, teachers, on the other hand, need to choose the sources to be used as input, basing their choices on two areas: (a) the frequency and difficulty of the words for their students and (b) the interests of the particular students. Depending on the students' proficiency, teachers may compile and concord materials for beginning students, then go on to train more advanced students to compile and concord their own material. Kennedy and Miceli (2001), however, in teaching a group of intermediate learners of Italian who were working with a corpus of contemporary written Italian, found that many of the students' problems with the concordancing task stemmed not from lack of language proficiency but from their being inadequately prepared to "acquire certain attitudes and habits of researching" (p. 87). That is, Kennedy and Miceli suggest that teachers invest time up front marketing the observations that can come from mining such a language database.

The relevance of word frequency, the first consideration in choosing vocabulary material, has been extensively studied by Paul Nation and an affiliated group of scholars in New Zealand. Describing Nation's 1990 book *Teaching and Learning Vocabulary*, Cobb (2002) summarizes the state of frequency studies:

> Computer analysis shows that about 80% of the individual words in most written English texts are members of the 2000 most frequent word families, so that any second language reading course should ensure that its users meet and know these words. After roughly the 2000 mark, however, the pay off for direct learning trails off, and at that point learners should either rely on inferencing strategies or else move on to direct study of items that are frequent not in the language at large but in chosen areas of study or interest such as academic texts in general or domains of study like economics in particular. Either way, the goal is to arrive at a point where 95% of the running words are known in an average text, which a series of experiments show is the point where independent reading and further acquisition through inference become reliable. (p. 243)

For teachers seeking information on the words in a given text, Nation and Coxhead have produced the software *Range* (formerly *Fvords* and *VocabProfile*) and *Frequency*–Windows programs for analyzing lexical distribution in texts. Studies of the 2,000 most frequent words were first set forth in a list of "general service" words compiled by West (1953); while more recently, lists of words in academic English have been compiled by Xue and Nation (1984) and Coxhead (2000).

The second aspect in choosing texts to input, which involves connecting to the reader's background knowledge and interest in the topic, is also known to be important in motivating readers. Specifically, reading teachers are encouraged to activate readers' "schema" (Carrell & Eisterhold, 1983; Carrell, 1984) by either bringing them up to speed on necessary background concepts, or first encouraging them to recall what they may already know on a topic. Either way, students are more inclined to keep acquiring new terms and increasing their reading speed if they have some initial interest in or need to know more about a given subject. Thus, teachers are encouraged to either have some say in the selection of appropriate reading materials, or even to let readers choose their own. This supports the idea of using specialized corpora from which to cull new vocabulary. If students are engaged in learning and writing outside of class on the topics of chemistry or folktales, for example, then readings on history or sports may not make the most motivating vocabulary sources, and vice versa. Accessing a general language corpus is also less likely to reveal the relevant uses of the terms that students need to acquire in their chosen areas of reading.

Many English as a Second Language reference books and teacher training texts have begun to acknowledge the need to incorporate concordancing and frequency tabulating technology, but often in a preliminary way. Three books are examined here, as being typical of the different types of areas that teacher texts focus on. The first, represented by Omaggio Hadley (2001), is a general methodology textbook for teachers of ESL. The author devotes two pages to a section discussing how computers can provide "richer content for language learning" (p. 163) but cites only two works, both from 1998, that present an overview of technology issues in language study. These highlight ways to use authentic material, including the Web, and caution about the need for teacher input, though no particular analytical tools are presented. Thus the issue of the pedagogical impact of technology is raised, but the interested teacher must seek details elsewhere. Anderson (1999), in a book that focuses just on reading skills, goes a bit further. This author discusses the potential benefits of using indexing software in vocabulary studies, mentioning the DOS program VocabProfile, and going on to include a suggestion that readers download MonoConc and try it on a text being used for a reading class (pp. 31-32). These are more specific starting points, but the coverage in the text is quite brief, and the software mentioned is neither free, platform independent, nor current. Finally, Boswood (1997) edits a useful handbook of short, hands-on classroom techniques. He includes six concordancing selections by different authors, which look at such topics as collecting commonly co-occurring word pairs, developing vocabulary, creating corpora, and learning to do concordancing. This book is more focused, but assumes a familiarity with the software being discussed, as in these instructions for setting up a concordancing lesson on overused vocabulary words: "Procedure: 1. Instruct the students in the use of the concordancer if necessary. . . . " (p. 266). Despite such rudimentary coverage in general Teaching of English as Second Language books, many other works specifically focusing on issues of computers in language learning are available for those who are already intending to incorporate such technology (as seen in specialist subsets of professional organizations, such as the Computer Assisted Language Learning Interest Section [CALL-IS] of the professional group Teachers of English to Speakers of Other Languages or the Computer Studies in Language and Literature Discussion Group of the Modern Language Association). Many uninitiated teachers, however, may be surprised to find how easily such technology tools fit into their existing teaching goals.

FINDING THE TOOLS

Having decided to attempt a data-driven approach to vocabulary instruction, where does a teacher find the two necessary software types–the corpora themselves and the concordancing programs? Several issues are involved in acquiring these tools.

First, as far as the collection of texts to sample, many bodies of texts are available already, free or to purchase, on CD or via download. Of course, to end up with a corpus specific to a given class, one attractive option is to compile one's own texts. Getting texts into electronic form is easier than it once was. Typing and downloading are the most likely methods, with scanning and optical character recognition, or inputting via voice recognition software as additional possibilities. (See Bowker & Pearson [2002] for details, however, as these latter methods can be more time consuming than they first appear, and generally require additional software as well.) Material on the Web, as mentioned earlier, can be mined for public domain sources such as the fiction being continually added to Project Gutenberg, selections of e-mail postings and chat, professional journalism sites, and so on, although another caveat is that many of these will be copyrighted. Once a teacher has selected the appropriate texts to work with, another consideration is whether the corpus should be "tagged," where tagged means that each word's part of speech is labeled. Clearly, there are advantages to having a text that is already tagged for part of speech (so that, for example, students can hunt for just the verb *run*, rather than the noun *run*, or check for a suffix that attaches only to a certain class of word, such as the *-ly* that attaches to adjectives in order to form adverbs, as found in *quickly*, and *suddenly*, rather than the less frequent *-ly* that attaches to nouns to form adjectives, as found in *ghostly* and *friendly*). However, the likelihood is that most teachers and students will have available to them only untagged texts. In fact, the sorting of similar looking word forms is one of the tasks that students would then be able to profitably perform themselves. (Not to mention the difficulties in finding one set of tags that all users would agree on and be fluent in. Most text tagging is done by linguists rather than language teachers, and hence contains much finer, and often more cryptic, distinctions than the familiar "principal parts of speech" that students first encounter. When doing their first-hand tagging exercise, even computational linguistics graduate students are often initially overwhelmed by the options provided by the 65-180 members of various tag sets.)

After a corpus has been obtained, the second step is to try out some concordancing and indexing software tools on the texts. Many sources exist for specially designed software for concordancing and indexing texts. Mike Scott's WordSmith Tools suite and Michael Barlow's MonoConc, for example, are both full of features and well supported, though both only run in a Windows environment. For Macintosh users, SIL's Conc and Mark Zimmermans's old HyperCard stack FreeText are both also packed with features, and have the additional advantage of being free. Users with little time or money to invest in new software skills, however, may find it is possible to start by accessing some concordance-like tools they already have at hand. For example, for concordancing abilities, those familiar with the UNIX environment may recognize that the command "grep" will scan for and gather all instances of a given token from a designated text file. Stevens (1995) contains a brief discussion of DOS commands that do likewise (p. 4), thus command line users have options available. For Windows and Macintosh users, the newest free version of Adobe Reader (6.0) now has a concordancing feature in its "find" function, so that a basic word search of any PDF file now brings up a small keyword in context list for the word.

As for tools that count and sort words, separate modules of the four concordance programs mentioned above each present windows that give a list of every different word in a text—ordered either alphabetically or in some cases by frequency. However, teachers who already have a word-processing or spreadsheet program should check the "sort" feature (found, for example, under the Table menu of Word and under the Data menu of Excel) which will allow one to sort a list of words alphabetically as well. And free indexing tools on the Web (e.g., Cathy Ball's Web Frequency Indexer) will also sort text that is pasted in, giving back a list sorted either by frequency or alphabetical order. By combining the output of these various free sorting programs, a teacher can readily get a list of high- or low-frequency words in a given text selection, and from this information, select relevant terms with which the students can run a concordance search to then try working out the meanings from contextual and linguistic clues.

The sections discussed here have pointed out the Type II aspects of using specialized text corpora and concordancing tools to help students improve vocabulary learning in a second language. This student-centered, data-driven learning method can be easily adapted for different levels of reading students. Students will benefit by getting practice in observation and critical thinking as well as language mastery itself. Teachers are encouraged to try out ways of acquiring electronic copies of texts containing specialized authentic language as well as finding sources of tools for sorting and concordancing these texts.

REFERENCES

Adobe Reader (Version 6.0) [Computer software]. (2004). Adobe Systems Incorporated. http://www.adobe.com/products/acrobat/readstep2.html

Anderson, N. (1999). *Exploring second language reading: Issues and strategies.* Boston: Heinle & Heinle.

Ball, C. Web Frequency Indexer [Computer software]. Georgetown University. http://www.georgetown.edu/cball/webtools/web_freqs.html

Biber, D., Johansson, S., Leech, G., Conrad, S., & Finegan, E. (1999). *Longman grammar of spoken and written English.* Harlow, UK: Longman.

Boswood, T. (Ed.). (1997). *New ways of using computers in language teaching.* Alexandria, VA: Teachers of English to Speakers of Other Languages, Inc.

Bowker, L., & Pearson, J. (2002). *Working with specialized language: A practical guide to using corpora.* London/New York: Routledge.

CALL-IS. Computer Assisted Language Learning Interest Section of TESOL. http://www.uoregon.edu/~call/

Carrell, P. L. (1984). Schema theory and ESL reading: Classroom implications and applications. *The Modern Language Journal, 68*(4), 332-343.

Carrell, P. L., & Eisterhold, J. (1983). Schema theory and ESL reading pedagogy. *TESOL Quarterly, 17*, 553-573.

Cobb, T. (2002). Review of Paul Nation, Learning vocabulary in another language. *Canadian Journal of Linguistics, 46*(3/4), 242-245.

Cobb, T. (2004). Is there any measurable learning from hands-on concordancing? *System, 25*(3), 301-315.

Conc (Version 1.80b3) [Computer software]. (1996). SIL International. http://www. sil.org/computing/catalog/show_software.asp?id=9

Coxhead, A. (2000). A new academic wordlist. *TESOL Quarterly, 34*(2), 213-238.

Francis, W. N., & Kucera, H. (1967). Brown Corpus [CD ROM text collection]. The ICAME Corpus Collection.

Ghadessy, M., Henry, A., & Roseberry, R. L. (Eds.). (2001). *Small corpus studies and ELT: Theory and practice.* Amsterdam: John Benjamins.

Granger, S. (1998). The computer learner corpus: A testbed for electronic EFL tools. In J. Nerbonne (Ed.), *Linguistic databases* (pp. 175-188). Stanford, CA: CSLI Publications.

Hadley, G. (2002). Sensing the winds of change: An introduction to data-driven learning. *RELC Journal: A Journal of Language Teaching and Research in Southeast Asia, 33*(2), 99-124.

Johns, T. (1994). From printout to handout: Grammar and vocabulary teaching in the context of data-driven learning. In T. Odlin (Ed.), *Perspectives on pedagogical grammar* (pp. 293-313). New York: Cambridge University Press.

Kennedy, C., & Miceli, T. (2001). An evaluation of intermediate students' approaches to corpus investigation. *Language Learning and Technology, 5*(3), 77-90.

Maddux, C. D., Johnson, D. L., & Willis, J. W. (2001). *Educational computing: Learning with tomorrow's technologies* (3rd ed.). Boston: Allyn & Bacon.

Miller, G. A., & Gildea, P. M. (1987, September). How children learn words. *Scientific American*, 86.

MLA. Modern Language Association. http://www.mla.org/

Monoconc [Computer software]. http://www.monoconc.com/. Houston, TX: Athelson Software.

Nation, I. S. P. (1990). *Teaching and learning vocabulary.* Boston: Heinle & Heinle.

Nation, I. S. P. Frequency [Computer software]. http://www.vuw.ac.nz/lals/about/software. aspx

Nation, I. S. P. Range [Computer software]. http://www.vuw.ac.nz/lals/about/software. aspx

Omaggio Hadley, A. (2001). *Teaching language in context* (3rd ed.). Boston: Heinle & Heinle.

Project Gutenberg. (2004). [Online text collection]. http://www.gutenberg.net/

Scott, M. WordSmith Tools (Version 4.0) [Computer software]. Oxford University Press. http://www.lexically.net/wordsmith/

Sinclair, J. (1987). *Collins COBUILD English language dictionary.* London: Collins.

Stevens, V. (1995). Concordancing with language learners: Why? when? what? *CAELL Journal, 6*(2), 2-10.

Trados Freelance (Version 6.5) [Computer software]. WinAlign features detailed at http://www.trados.com/offer/prz/t6new.html

Tribble, C. (1997). *Improvising corpora for ELT: Quick-and-dirty ways of developing corpora for language teaching.* Paper presented at the Practical Applications in Language Corpora (PALC), Lodz, Poland.

Tribble, C. (2001a). Corpora and corpus analysis: New windows on academic writing. In J. Flowerdew (Ed.), *Academic discourse* (pp. 131-149). Harlow, UK: Addison Wesley Longman.

Tribble, C. (2001b). Small corpora and teaching writing: Towards a corpus-informed pedagogy of writing. In M. Ghadessy, A. Henry, & R. L. Roseberry (Eds.), *Small corpus studies and ELT* (pp. 381-408). Amsterdam: John Benjamins.

Warschauer, M. (1996). Computer-assisted language learning: An introduction. In S. Fotos (Ed.), *Multimedia language teaching* (pp. 3-20). Tokyo: Logos International.

Warschauer, M. (1998). Researching technology in TESOL: Determinist, instrumental, and critical approaches. *TESOL Quarterly, 32*(4), 757-761.

West, M. (1953). *A general service list of English words.* London: Longman.

Woolls, D. (1996). Multiconcord (Version 4.1) [Computer software]. Birmingham: CFL Software Development. http://artsweb.bham.ac.uk/pking/multiconc/cfl.htm

Xue, G., & Nation, I. S. P. (1984). A university word list. *Language Learning and Communication, 32*, 215-219.

Zimmerman, M. (1988). FreeText Browser [Computer software].

Kulwadee Kongrith
Cleborne D. Maddux

Online Learning as a Demonstration of Type II Technology: Second-Language Acquisition

SUMMARY. Online learning can be an effective tool in second-language acquisition (SLA) because it can be an efficient and convenient way to provide accurate, understandable material to second-language learners. It is crucial for instructors to have online knowledge and skills as well as the ability to choose how, when, and to whom to apply such expertise. Online learning also promotes student-centered learning, which is widely believed to be important in SLA. Online learning technologies also have the advantage of reducing learner anxiety by providing a nonjudgmental, independent learning environment. In addition, SLA students using online learning may develop improved attitudes toward the second language (L2) and its culture. *[Article copies available for a fee from The Haworth Document Delivery Service: 1-800-HAWORTH. E-mail address: <docdelivery@haworthpress.com> Website:*

KULWADEE KONGRITH is a doctoral student, Department of Counseling and Educational Psychology, College of Education, University of Nevada, Reno, Reno, NV 89557 (E-mail: kulwadee@unr.edu).
CLEBORNE D. MADDUX is Associate Editor for Research, *Computers in the Schools*, and Foundation Professor, Department of Counseling and Educational Psychology, University of Nevada, Reno, Reno, NV 89557 (E-mail: maddux@unr.edu).

[Haworth co-indexing entry note]: "Online Learning as a Demonstration of Type II Technology: Second Language Acquisition." Kongrith, Kulwadee, and Cleborne D. Maddux. Co-published simultaneously in *Computers in the Schools* (The Haworth Press, Inc.) Vol. 22, No. 1/2, 2005, pp. 97-110; and: *Internet Applications of Type II Uses of Technology in Education* (ed: Cleborne D. Maddux, and D. LaMont Johnson) The Haworth Press, Inc., 2005, pp. 97-110. Single or multiple copies of this article are available for a fee from The Haworth Document Delivery Service [1-800-HAWORTH, 9:00 a.m. - 5:00 p.m. (EST). E-mail address: docdelivery@haworthpress.com].

Available online at http://www.haworthpress.com/web/CITS
© 2005 by The Haworth Press, Inc. All rights reserved.
Digital Object Identifier: 10.1300/J025v22n01_09

<http://www.HaworthPress.com> © 2005 by The Haworth Press, Inc. All rights reserved.]

KEYWORDS. Online second language acquisition, a second-language acquisition, online learning, English as a second language, foreign language learning, Type II technology, WebQuest, WebCT

Many technologies have been used as teaching and learning tools in education. Computers may be unique in their potential to improve teaching and learning (Maddux, Johnson, & Willis, 2001). Like any tool, the value of computers as learning tools depends on the tasks to which they are applied and how well they are used in pursuit of selected goals.

Maddux, Johnson, and Willis (2001) distinguish between the use of Type I and Type II educational computer applications. Type I educational applications are used to make it quicker, easier, and more efficient to continue teaching traditional topics in traditional ways. Type II educational applications, on the other hand, are designed to make available new and better ways of teaching. While there is nothing wrong with Type I applications, computers are so expensive–in terms of time, effort, and enthusiasm needed to bring them into classrooms–that this considerable investment can only be justified by the development and use of Type II applications in teaching and learning. Type II applications (a) incorporate a high degree of interactivity between computer and learner, (b) put the user rather than the software developer in charge of what happens on the screen, (c) are aimed at accomplishing relatively more creative tasks than are Type I applications, and (d) make possible the accomplishment of highly complex tasks (Maddux, Johnson, & Willis, 2001). From these characteristics, it seems apparent that online learning has the potential to be a Type II application of technology.

The history of computers in education goes back more than two decades. Initial applications were often referred to as computer-assisted instruction (CAI) or computer-based instruction (CBI) (Gibbons & Fairweather, 1998; Muth & Alvermann, 1999). The focus was often primarily on rote learning through drill-and-practice software. Kearsley (2000) suggests that the idea of computer-assisted learning was to provide an individualized learning experience. However, these early computer implementations did not provide the high-quality interaction that could be provided by traditional instruction involving teachers. While drill-and-practice forms of CAI were effective in producing achievement gains in some students (Muth & Alvermann, 1999), students quickly became bored with the rote nature of their involvement, and teachers became disillusioned with computers as effective learning tools that could be applied to important teaching and learning problems.

In the early 1990s, the World Wide Web became widely available. The Web made it easy to create, interrelate, and access vast amounts of information, eventually in multimedia format. Moreover, it brought together a variety of electronic interactive formats including e-mail, chat groups, threaded discussions, and conferencing. The Web's multimedia capabilities made it possible to engage students through the use of graphics, sound, and video (Kearsley, 2000).

Computer technologies have now become important in education. In the United States, virtually every classroom now has access to the Internet. In 1997, the White House announced four goals for education, one of which was for effective software and online learning resources to become an integral part of every school's curriculum by the year 2000 (Muth & Alvermann, 1999).

Online learning is now widely available and has expanded into many different subjects, including second-language teaching. Some courses are offered completely online, while others use online learning to supplement traditional classroom teaching. According to Allen (1999), most online courses that promote writing skills include the following elements:

1. *Lecture*. Lectures can be delivered via a Web site or e-mail and are basically a reading assignment.
2. *Readings*. Reading materials can be posted on a Web site.
3. *Discussion*. Online learning can bring the entire class together in a chat room for real-time discussions.
4. *Homework*. Homework assignments can be posted on the course Web site or delivered via e-mail, and the instructor can ask students to post or share their homework assignments for class critiquing.
5. *Individual feedback*. Instructors will generally provide detailed comments on students' homework assignments and will also be available to answer the questions personally through e-mail. If students post a question that would benefit the entire class, the instructor can easily distribute the question and responses to the entire class via e-mail.

HOW CAN ONLINE LEARNING BE AN EFFECTIVE TOOL IN SECOND-LANGUAGE ACQUISITION?

Online learning can be beneficial for second-language acquisition (SLA) learners. It requires basic writing and communication skills and provides practice in written communication. This is important because written and oral communication skills are major components in SLA.

According to Neri, Cucchiarini, Strik, and Boves (2002) the basic ingredient for successful language acquisition is input. Online learning can be used to provide "comprehensible input," which refers to language used in ways that make it understandable to the learner even though second-language proficiency is limited (Krashen, 1983; Peregoy & Boyle, 2001). Comprehensible input can be provided by online learning in both formal and informal ways. Cook (1996) explains Krashen's "input hypothesis," which is that linguistic knowledge consists of both acquired knowledge and learned knowledge.

Brown (1994) refers to Krashen's belief that fluency in second-language performance is due to what one has acquired. Acquired knowledge is gained by natural means in informal situations (a process termed *acquisition*). "Acquisition is a subconscious, intuitive process of constructing the system of a language" (Brown, 1994, p. 279). This is the source of all first-language knowledge and some second-language knowledge. Acquired knowledge consists of rules, principles, etc., that are not consciously perceived.

Learned knowledge is gained by conscious understanding of rules. This is the form of second-language knowledge acquired in formal classroom situations. "Learning language is *knowledge about* language, *formal knowledge* of a language" (Krashen, 1983, p. 26).

Neri et al. (2002) suggest that input has to be meaningful to a learner. Learners should feel that materials are relevant to their needs. Teachers often report improvements in writing and communications skills as a consequence of the online experience (Kearsley, 2000). This may be due to the increased relevancy present when students use e-mail to communicate with others. Then, too, e-mail and other computer writing tasks are attractive for use with second-language learners, especially for beginners and introverted students, because they may feel more comfortable writing than they do speaking a second language. This is true because they do not have to confront the teacher and other students while they are communicating, and because they know they can go back to correct errors. Then, too, when writing rather than speaking, students have more time to think and compose.

Schwarz (1988) investigated anxiety in second-language classrooms. He found that independent study helps eliminate anxiety because students are not called upon to perform before their peers. This is important because second-language students may feel reluctant to talk in the presence of native speakers, particularly when their second-language proficiencies are limited. They are afraid of making errors and self-conscious about speaking more slowly than in their own language because they need time to translate from their native language to the second language. In traditional classrooms, the extroverted and advanced students often dominate the classroom discussions. Perhaps chat room discussions would allow for more participation by second-language students who may be reluctant to share their views in a face-to-face classroom.

Another advantage is that e-mail and other computer writing tasks encourage self-monitoring because of the ability to proofread before producing a final draft. Proofreading may encourage SLA students to review grammatical rules, recheck spelling, and rethink the concept of the context. Then, too, e-mailing provides strong motivation since students want their best work to go to their instructors. The students always have choices to respond to messages or questions when they are ready, and this can provide opportunities to learn anywhere and anytime.

Online classes can be set up to deliver messages to students via a Web site or e-mail. However, it is crucial for teachers in such situations to assure that students receive messages and respond to those messages. Teachers also need to build in opportunities to provide students with feedback on their writing, and provide times when students are helped to correct errors.

Another reason that online learning can be particularly effective in second-language acquisition is that it can provide learners with autonomy and the choice of when, where, and how to study (Kearsley, 2000). "This allows learners increased freedom to pursue their own interests as well as methods of learning" (Kearsley, 2000, p. 62). This freedom may promote independent learning and allow learners to make use of their own effective learning strategies. For example, some students concentrate better when they work alone, and use of a computer for such students can be a definite advantage.

While e-mail and other computer writing applications are beneficial, there are also many foreign language sites and resources available on the Internet that allow for self-study by anyone who is interested in a given language. They are easy to access by students who want to start an in-depth study of a second language or by those who want to learn only a few words and phrases (Thomas, 2000). Thomas also suggests Web sites that can help learners become bilingual. For example, if students want to learn a few phrases in French, Spanish, Italian, or German, it is easy to access the tutorials on http://www.fodors.com/language/. For Russian, Portuguese, Icelandic, and about 70 other languages, tutorials are available at http://www.Travlang.com. About 60% of the online words have audio files with pronunciations (Joseph, 1999). There is also a real-time voice service called Lipstream, which allows students and instructors to conduct voice discussions (Cupertino, 2001). Participants can talk from PC to PC or PC to phone where audio Internet access is unavailable.

Online learning provides a setting where students can discuss theory and research issues without being threatened by the established social order (Matsuda, 2002). In addition, Li (2000) found that students wrote with a higher level of syntactic and lexical complexity in nonstructured e-mail tasks than in the structured ones. When the students were given more freedom and control of their learning activities, they used more sophisticated language in their writing.

Motivation is important in second-language acquisition. There are two types of motivation: integrative and instrumental motivation. Integrative motivation refers to whether the student identifies with, or rejects, the target culture and people. There is a relationship between admiration of the target culture and success in SLA. The more students admire the target culture (as demonstrated by reading its literature or looking for opportunities to practice the language), the more successful students will be in SLA. Instrumental motivation is learning the language for reasons unconnected to its use with native speakers; for example, to pass an examination or to obtain a better job (Cook, 1996).

Online learning often proves to be more enjoyable than traditional classes for students by allowing them to study topics of interest to them. For example, listening to songs may lead to increased interest by students in SLA. Such students may become more proficient in a second language because they first enjoy listening to songs in the target language and become interested in learning the meaning of the lyrics.

Positive attitudes toward the second language and the culture from which it came are related to the eventual success in learning the language (Brown, 1994). Thus, it is important for instructors to provide experiences that encourage students to have positive attitudes toward the target culture. Schwartz (1988) points out a related advantage of online learning: Students can review difficult lessons, drills, and exercises as often as they like since the computer will not become inpatient as an instructor might. Thus, the second-language learner using online learning may be more likely to have a positive attitude toward SLA than those students in traditional face-to-face settings. Due to the interactive nature of SLA, it is inevitable that the learner will learn some of the culture associated with the second language (Liaw & Johnson, 2001). Understanding and acceptance of other cultures are key pedagogical aims for foreign language education (Liaw & Johnson, 2001). An example according to Liaw and Johnson (2001) involves cross-cultural e-mail correspondence, which they assert can sensitize the participants to cultural differences and serve as a bridge to better cross-cultural understanding.

Online learning can also be valuable because it can promote a student-centered approach to SLA, allowing for self-paced learning styles, and increased risk-taking (D'Aquila, 1999). Because there is a student-centered learning environment, students are responsible for contributing to their own education (Muth & Alvermann, 1999, p. 276). For example, in English as a Second Language (ESL) classes, the instructors might divide students into groups of three to four students to discuss topics involving American culture. Students can engage in online brainstorming activities, deciding what they will discuss and how in depth their discussion will be without being inhibited by their perceived poor second-language skills. Students can e-mail back and forth among the group members, which may lead to increased knowledge of curriculum topics. Students can choose a leader to coordinate the collection of the needed information. Then, they can assign members to look for specific information and decide how the data will be presented. This activity will require students to communicate using the bulletin board or e-mail. Concurrently, "students engaged in inquiry projects may e-mail their questions to subject-area experts around the world" (Muth & Alvermann, 1999, p. 202). By preparing papers on the target culture, students must use strategies such as repeated reading, planning and organizing their data collection, researching, engaging in cooperative learning, and creating analogies. Students use these strategies on their own without the help of the instructor (Muth & Alvermann, 1999).

Giving students clear and clean instructions is important in student-centered learning. There are many interesting activities that teachers can create through online learning in SLA. For instance, teachers can have students participate in collaborative Internet projects with other ESL classrooms or pre-service bilingual/ESL teachers around the world.

Ogata, Feng, Hada, and Yano (2000) tested a Communicative Collection Assisting System (CoCoA) to promote *student-centered instructing* and learning for foreign students learning Japanese written composition. They concluded that the CoCoA system could be used as a spelling and grammar check for foreign students' writing compositions in Japanese. It was also easy for the students to understand the teacher's corrections in their compositions because the corrections were typed as opposed to handwritten. The CoCoA also supports feedback messages of the morphological error profile (grammatical correction feature) and the exercises of writing error correction were effective in facilitating the learning of second-language writing.

Teaching and learning grammar can be very time consuming. Students need to spend time outside the classroom to practice, use, and memorize grammatical rules. Nielsen and Carlsen (2003) note that the learner is more confident in the use of specific rules when structured grammar drills and exercises take place outside the classroom. Online learning can be used as a grammar interactive tool in SLA, even for difficult languages such as Arabic (a language written in non-roman scripts). Nielsen and Carlsen (2003) used an Internet-based interactive software package for self-paced learning of Arabic grammar. Students were able to analyze Arabic sentences by using Arabic script and Arabic grammatical terminology.

Online learning in SLA can also be useful because of its entertainment value (D'Aquila, 1999). Because it is entertaining, online learning has the potential to increase student motivation. Hird (2000) suggests that it is no surprise that the Internet has entertainment appeal, especially for teens, because it provides easy access to information of interest to them. Such information is related to movies, music stars, and sports. If these subjects are provided in a second language, the students may enjoy the experience while becoming more proficient in SLA. Krashen (1983) suggests that having fun in SLA reduces negative attitudes, and thus may be considered an "affective filter" in SLA (Krashen, 1983). According to the affective filter hypothesis, one of Krashen's five hypotheses in SLA, people acquire a second language when their affective filters are favorable enough to allow for comprehensive input (Peregoy & Boyle, 2001).

Online learning is communication using all four language skills: writing, reading, listening, and speaking (such as when using audio files). Online learning lessons can be designed to use all these skills. Peregoy and Boyle (2001) state that listening to and understanding spoken language are essential components in SLA.

Online tasks should be interesting and challenging to the students. Egbert (2003) defines flow experiences as a balance between challenge and skills, and suggests that flow experiences can lead to optimal learning. Online learning can support "flow" experiences through providing repetition, motivation, exploration, satisfaction, more time on task, and willingness to risk. Egbert (2003) notes that such students are better motivated to repeat and accomplish tasks at a more challenging level. As the students become more proficient, the difficulty level increases to further challenge them.

Another advantage of online learning in second-language instruction is that it can be made highly social. Students can interact with other students and the instructor. With audio-capable computers, they can even speak to one another and a high degree of autonomy can still be maintained. Interactive learning is authentic learning:

> Even though students have no physical presence in the space created on the Internet, they *see* and *hear* each other as though they were engaged in face-to-face communication and interaction in the same room. As their minds meet through digital communication, the students engage in relationships and activities that are as real to them as anything they do in their physically defined habitats. (Hird, 2000, p. 47)

Liaw (1998) investigated the efficacy of integrating e-mail writing into two English as a Foreign Language (EFL) classrooms and explored the social dynamics involved in the process of e-mail exchanges. Liaw (1998) suggests that the use of e-mail required the students to use English to communicate with another second-language speaker and that acquiring computer skills was a valuable experience for many students. The study showed social interaction was a major driving force for active communication between partners. Liaw (1998) concluded that effective integration of e-mail writing into the second-language classrooms facilitated SLA.

Interactive online learning also benefits teachers, since they can provide corrective feedback to individuals immediately via writing. Glasgow and Hicks (2003) suggest that feedback is more meaningful when delivered in an appropriate way. The corrective feedback is personal so it will not make the student embarrassed. Neri et al. (2002), using computer-assisted pronunciation training, found that the system should provide input, output, and feedback. They further suggested that the system should provide students with corrective feedback to help learners notice the discrepancies between their output and the second language. However, feedback should not be limited to identifying a student's response as right or wrong, and should provide numerous suggestions for changes.

Furthermore, using a chat room mediated discussion at certain times can facilitate interaction between students and instructors. Students can post a question and respond to other participants' opinions in real time. To encourage native speakers and non-native speakers to participate in the chat room, the instructor might include students in another language class. For example, in the United States, a Spanish class and an ESL class could collaborate and interact with one another. Then, too, a classroom at a public school could be set up to facilitate the communication between two native-speaking classes of different languages. Having a native speaker as a pen pal is an interesting and fun online activity in SLA, and students may gain both the language and knowledge about the target culture. It is easy to keep in touch online, since e-mail can be sent and responded to when it is convenient for both parties. Problems with different time zones are eliminated. Long and Porter (1985) found that the give and take of conversations between native and non-native speakers is a crucial element of the language-acquisition process (as cited in Peregoy & Boyle, 2001).

There are many other online learning options that support the effectiveness of online learning as a tool in SLA. For example, instructors can provide linked Web pages containing traditional classroom content, such as lecture notes and syllabi, as well as readings that students can access on the Web. WebQuests and WebCT are good examples of online learning technologies that can be used both inside and outside of classrooms. Discussion boards, private mail, and chat rooms can be easily created using WebCT and can help students communicate with their classmates and instructors. Hwu (2003) points out that WebCT's tracking system can be a useful device for teachers to monitor students' behaviors and to determine which activities need to be improved to better serve students' needs.

It is important to understand that acquiring a second language is not simply a matter of obtaining a body of knowledge. A language learner requires more than access to lecture notes and readings with traditional objective tests and quizzes. E-mail, discussion boards, and chat rooms offer learners a forum for using the target language as a communicative tool (Wible, Kuo, Chien, Liu, & Tsao, 2001). Wible et al. (2001) created an online writing environment that connects teachers and students, via a user-friendly interface, to provide ways to exploit the valuable interaction that is created in this autonomous environment. They concluded:

An authoring environment for online help permits content administrators to turn interlanguage research results into highly specific help concerning attested difficulties which traditional language education has neglected. It is hoped that increasingly sophisticated and dynamic manipulations of these sorts of data will lead to the delivery of evermore useful and useable information to learners, teachers, and researchers both online and off. (p. 315)

WebQuests were developed by Bernie Dodge and Tom March at San Diego State University in 1995. Dodge (1997) defines a WebQuest as "an inquiry-oriented activity in which some or all of the information that learners interact with comes from resources on the Internet, optionally supplemented with videoconferencing" (p. 1). The WebQuest is an excellent vehicle to provide authentic communication for second-language students in using technology in the classroom. It is also a viable alternative to traditional pedagogy and allows the teacher to select the appropriate sites and keep the students on task.

Kongrith (2001) investigated the efficacy of integrating a WebQuest into an ESL classroom and explored the attitudes of the ESL students toward using that WebQuest. First, the students read the book *Of Mice and Men* and then participated in a WebQuest. The results from the attitude survey indicated that the book was much harder for students to understand than the sites provided in the WebQuest. The book employs a great deal of slang and other dialogue, which second-language learners found difficult to understand. The WebQuest provided the meaning of the slang words in each chapter and included a summary of each chapter.

CONCLUSION

Online learning may hold the power to create learning environments rich with opportunities for students to develop communicative competence while providing authentic communication. The World Wide Web offers many opportunities to develop these skills.

Second-language learners need comprehensible inputs to be able to succeed in SLA. Affective filters are major barriers that can block students from SLA. In other words, if students have negative attitudes toward the second language and its culture, or experience high anxiety or poor motivation while in a traditional classroom, they may experience poor results in SLA.

Online learning can be an effective tool in SLA because it can provide comprehensible input. Moreover, students experience less anxiety while learning independently with online learning technologies and are likely to be highly motivated while using these technologies in SLA. In addition, online learning promotes a student-centered learning approach (Kearsley, 2000). Students also can monitor themselves while taking online quizzes. They can often go back to see where they made mistakes and correct them. Also, since online learning provides autonomy, they will be much more likely to use new words and more complex sentences since the fear of embarrassing themselves in front of a class is eliminated. Therefore, students may be more likely to become language risk-taking learners.

Second-language learners are most likely to be more effective learners in SLA if they are provided with particularly meaningful lessons. Muth and Alvermann (1999) concluded that "by offering students with special needs various ways of expressing themselves, technology has the potential to motivate even the hardest-to-reach students and to open up new avenues of learning for students who speak English as a second language" (p. 208).

According to Richards and Rodgers (1996), surfing the Web can sometimes be difficult in a second language. Also, keeping students on task is a challenge in any class. Teachers can make it a much more enjoyable and constructive experience by providing an instructional framework for them. Interactive computing can make language learning more natural by matching and more closely approximating the real functions of communication (Muth & Alvermann, 1999). In conclusion, online learning can be an effective tool for both students and instructors who know how, when, and with whom to use it.

REFERENCES

Allen, M. A. (1999). *Writing.com*. New York: Allworth Press.

Brown, H. (1994). *Principles of language learning and teaching* (3rd ed). Englewood Cliffs, NJ: Prentice Hall.

Cook, V. (1996). *Second language learning and language teaching* (2nd ed). New York: Arnold.

Cupertino, C. (2001). *Lipstream brings real-time voice service to cultura inglesa online language courses*. Retrieved February 15, 2002, from http://www.findarticles.com/cf_0/m4PRN/2001_April_19/73387621/p1/article.jhtml

D'Aquila, L. C. (1999). Computer-assisted language learning toward the national and New York State standards for German. *Dissertation Abstracts International, 60* (07), 2413A. (UMI No. 9936779)

Dodge, B. (1997). *Some thoughts about WebQuests.* Retrieved February 15, 2002, from http://edweb.sdsu.edu/courses/edtec596/about_webquests.html

Egbert, J. (2003). A study of flow theory in the foreign language classroom. *The Modern Language Journal, 87*(4), 499-518.

Gibbons, A., & Fairweather, P. (1998). *Designing computer based instruction.* Englewood Cliffs, NJ: Educational Technology Publications.

Glasgow, N. A., & Hicks, C. D. (2003). *What successful teachers do: 91 research-based classroom strategies for new and veteran teachers.* Thousand Oaks, CA: Corwin Press.

Hird, A. (2000). *Learning from cyber-savvy students: How Internet-age kids impact classroom teaching.* Sterling, VA: Stylus Publishing.

Hwu, F. (2003). Learners' behaviors in computer-based input activities elicited through tracking technologies. *Computer Assisted Language Learning, 16*(1), 5-29.

Joseph, C. (1999). *Net curriculum.* Medford, NJ: Information Today.

Kearsley, G. (2000). *Online education: Learning and teaching in cyberspace.* Stamford, CT: Thomson Learning.

Kongrith, K. *The ESL WebQuest for reading and writing skills: "Of Mice and Men."* Retrieved February 15, 2002, from: http://www.scs.unr.edu/~kongrith/

Krashen, S. (1983). *The natural approach: Language acquisition in the classroom.* Englewood Cliffs, NJ: Alemany Press.

Li, Y. (2000). Linguistic characteristics of ESL writing in task-based e-mail activities. *System, 28,* 229-245.

Liaw, M. L. (1998) Using electronic mail for English as a foreign language instruction. *System, 26,* 335-351.

Liaw, M. L., & Johnson, R. J. (2001). E-mail writing as a cross-cultural learning experience. *System, 29,* 235-251.

Maddux, C. D., Johnson, D. L., & Willis, J. W. (2001). *Educational computing: Learning with tomorrow's technologies* (3rd ed). Needham Heights, MA: Allyn & Bacon.

Matsuda, P. K. (2002). On negotiation of identity and power in a Japanese online discourse community. *Computers and Composition, 19,* 39-55.

Muth, K., & Alvermann, D. (1999). *Teaching and learning in the middle grades.* Needham Heights, MA: Allyn & Bacon.

Neri, A., Cucchiarini, C., Strik, H., & Boves, L. (2002). The pedagogy-technology interface in computer assisted pronunciation training. *Computer Assisted Language Learning, 15*(5), 441-467.

Nielsen, H. L., & Carlsen, M. (2003). Interactive Arabic grammar on the Internet: Problems and solutions. *Computer Assisted Language Learning, 16*(1), 95-112.

Ogata, H., Feng, C., Hada, Y., & Yano, Y. (2000). Online markup based language learning environment. *Computers & Education, 34,* 51-66.

Peregoy, S., & Boyle, O. (2001). *Reading, writing, and learning in ESL: A resource book for K-12 teachers* (3rd ed). New York: Addison Wesley Longman.

Richards, J., & Rodgers, T. (1996). *Approaches and methods in language teaching.* New York: Cambridge University Press.

Schwartz, M. (1988). Anxiety in the language classroom and computer-assisted language learning. *Dissertation Abstracts International, 50* (02), 434A. (UMI No. 8909011)

Thomas, P. (2000). *Study a foreign language online.* Retrieved February 15, 2001, from: http://www.findarticles.com/cf_0/m3337/6_17/70204200/p2/article.jhtml

Wible, D., Kuo, C.-H, Chien, F., Liu, A., & Tsao, N.-L. (2001). A Web-based EFL writing environment: Integrating information for learners, teachers, and researches. *Computers & Education, 37,* 297-315.

Ross Dewstow
Noeline Wright

Secondary School Students, Online Learning, and External Support in New Zealand

SUMMARY. Efforts combining online learning with classroom-based learning in secondary schools are not often reported. It is even more unusual to read reports detailing ways in which external experts can help both students and teachers learn "on the job" using both classroom and online facilities. This is particularly true in New Zealand, where teachers in secondary schools are beginning to understand the possibilities of online learning as an adjunct to normal classroom activities. This report describes a small project in which a secondary school teacher and her students learn about Web design as part of their ICT (information communication technologies) subject and work with an external expert from the local university. Within this project, the external expert acts as a facilitator for both the students' and the teacher's learning. *[Article copies available for a fee from The Haworth Document Delivery Service: 1-800-HAWORTH. E-mail address: <docdelivery@haworthpress.com>*

ROSS DEWSTOW is a Learning Designer, Ectus Ltd, Hamilton, New Zealand (E-mail: rdewstow@ectus.net).
NOELINE WRIGHT is a Researcher and Lecturer, WMIER & Department of Professional Studies in Education, School of Education, University of Waikato, Hamilton, New Zealand (E-mail: n.wright@waikato.ac.nz).

[Haworth co-indexing entry note]: "Secondary School Students, Online Learning, and External Support in New Zealand." Dewstow, Ross, and Noeline Wright. Co-published simultaneously in *Computers in the Schools* (The Haworth Press, Inc.) Vol. 22, No. 1/2, 2005, pp. 111-122; and: *Internet Applications of Type II Uses of Technology in Education* (ed: Cleborne D. Maddux, and D. LaMont Johnson) The Haworth Press, Inc., 2005, pp. 111-122. Single or multiple copies of this article are available for a fee from The Haworth Document Delivery Service [1-800-HAWORTH, 9:00 a.m. - 5:00 p.m. (EST). E-mail address: docdelivery@haworthpress.com].

Available online at http://www.haworthpress.com/web/CITS
© 2005 by The Haworth Press, Inc. All rights reserved.
Digital Object Identifier: 10.1300/J025v22n01_10

Website: <http://www.HaworthPress.com> © 2005 by The Haworth Press, Inc. All rights reserved.]

KEYWORDS. Online learning, classroom-based learning, ICT

INTRODUCTION

New Zealand has had Internet access since the University of Waikato established a gateway link in the late 1980s. While it was still rudimentary at that time, the School of Education within the university initiated Internet use with primary (elementary) schools in the region, to experiment with computer use in classrooms. Working with secondary schools has tended to be overlooked, partly because of their more complex organizational structures. It is only now, over a decade later, that most secondary schools have Internet access for both staff and students, and have begun working with the university on joint projects.

This growth in secondary schools' computer and Internet access has been accompanied by some central government-funded professional development programs over the last three years, intended to enhance both teachers' computer knowledge and skills and individuals' own desires to learn more. A report on this three-year funding period noted that the longer that teachers were involved, the more expert they became in information communication technologies (ICT) use and the more readily able they were to transfer their knowledge to active uses within classrooms (Ham, Gilmore, Kachelhoffer, Morrow, Moeau, & Wenmouth, 2002). Earlier, Ham (2001) had suggested that a key motivation for teachers to join in these ICT professional development programs was that they experienced a high degree of anxiety "about how to meet the needs of the media-savvy students arriving on their doorsteps" (p. 7).

A key stumbling block in the ability of teachers in New Zealand to become quickly comfortable with ICT and integration in their classrooms is that of time. Ham et al. (2002) noted the importance of this in their research. Even when teachers work daily within the field of ICT, the speed of technological changes often makes it hard for them to keep up to date, a point not lost on Maddux (1997), who noted a widening gap "between [the] sophistication of available technology and the faculty expertise to use it" (p. 5).

Since 1999, the University of Waikato has been developing its own online learning management system called *ClassForum*, based on the platform developed by Web Crossing. Throughout 2002, a version of ClassForum was used in a pilot project designed to test the usefulness of the system in both bridging the secondary school/tertiary education gap, and providing useful support for senior students in specific curriculum areas in local secondary schools.

An ICT teacher in one of these local schools later approached the director of the pilot project for support in helping students work on Web design as part of their curriculum. This teacher also wanted some of her students to enter a national secondary schools' Web-design competition. She could see the potential of the online system to provide support for the class and also increase her own expertise in using such a system for learning purposes.

This small-scale project is the focus of this article, but a discussion of the University of Waikato's online learning system, developed in-house, is required first.

CLASSFORUM: THE ONLINE LEARNING SYSTEM

Web Crossing is the underlying system used by the University of Waikato to generate its online learning management system, Class-Forum. A small team within the university has been involved in developing the system for educational uses, often prompted by individual lecturers wanting to replicate face-to-face classroom practices. This small team has now become an independent company that provides continuing online learning support to the university.

A key feature of this learning system is the sense of intimacy developed within an online classroom through the use of passport-sized photographs of every participant (both students and staff). These photographs accompany every posting individuals make. In this way, relationships between students and staff are enhanced. This is an attempt to replicate the face-to-face proximity experienced in classrooms when participants can see who they talk with and learn from. This feature encourages the kinds of collaboration and interaction Tu and Corry (2003) assert.

Another server is used to support all the external community and University of Waikato research projects that want to replicate the internal online learning system. This 'sister' system is called *Forum*. The separation of the internal (ClassForum) and external online learning systems (Forum) on different servers retains the integrity of the security of the internal online learning area because ClassForum is linked to the administration and student records databases. Forum was used with the secondary school students in the project under discussion here.

While the classroom teacher (Janice–a pseudonym) had some prior knowledge of ClassForum as a masters student with the University of Waikato's School of Education, she had no previous experience of creating any online structures or content. So, even though she and the students were therefore relatively new to the concept of teaching and learning online, they were prepared to take a risk with their learning. In preparing for the Web design topic and the online support to accompany it, the teacher used one of her holiday breaks to develop and construct the online area with the help of the external expert. At the same time, they kept in mind the goal of the Web design competition.

THE CLASS AND TEACHER

The students were a group of 16-17-year-olds in a girls' school's senior ICT class. All were confident using standard software on Windows-capable computers, but had not created any Web pages or worked with Web-editing or graphics software. While the classroom teacher was knowledgeable about various aspects of ICT, creating Web pages was a relatively new experience for her. She had limited skills in HTML (HyperText Markup Language), the software itself, and using any sort of file transfer programs to upload pages. This national Web page competition therefore not only tested students' knowledge and skills, but also that of the teacher. As is detailed later in this article, this initial lack of experience led to some problems, even though Janice had been working with these students on tasks that were more advanced than the advice Rekrut (1999) provided to teachers keen to use ICT in their classrooms. Rekrut suggested classroom teachers could begin introducing students to ICT by using e-mail. The students in this particular New Zealand class were already proficient users of e-mail, other ICT tools, and the Internet. The students' skills set cannot be ascribed only to the students' ages since theirs was not too different from Rekrut's grade 10 class. What may be more significant is both the greater access to technology these students have five years on from Rekrut's group, and their subject of ICT. This is a full-year class that built on skills and knowledge learned the previous year.

There was, however, still a great deal to learn. Designing Web pages was a new experience for all concerned. Janice therefore engaged in risk-taking along with students, suggesting both a great deal of openness and an effective student/teacher relationship where learning was co-operative and largely student-centered (Smeets & Mooij, 2001). The trial-and-error nature of the development of their skills in Web design, guided by the external expert/mentor in both virtual and face-to-face occasions, was a rich source of learning for all parties. And students quickly learned to communicate with the external expert as they sought advice in learning about Web design for the competition.

In other words, both the teacher and students developed their knowledge and understanding from working together through the scaffolded support and advice from the external expert. This fits within the parameters of the kind of socially oriented learning described by McInerney and McInerney (1998).

The developing pedagogical understanding of the teacher is also worth considering. Brown (1998) suggests that all teachers need different kinds of knowledge:

- General pedagogical knowledge
- Subject matter knowledge
- Domain-specific pedagogical knowledge
- ICT general and specific pedagogical knowledge and,
- Specific curriculum knowledge (p. 8).

In terms of a teacher of ICT, three of these categories merge: that of subject matter knowledge, ICT general and specific pedagogical knowledge, and specific curriculum knowledge. Given that ICT developments continue to be rapid, a teacher's ability to be ahead of these innovations for pedagogical purposes is problematic. Being able to call on someone else to help overcome this problem is ventrally important here.

THE EXTERNAL EXPERT

The external expert had a background in both secondary teaching and tertiary teaching. The tertiary teaching centered on the field of interactive media and Web design, while his secondary teaching background helped him understand the learning levels and degrees of challenge required for this class. The role the external expert played with the teacher and class was to guide and support, rather than take charge. In other words, he responded to needs and provided advice when it was sought. He was very clear in ensuring his role was that of guide and mentor, to empower both teacher and students in their learning journey so that, eventually, they would become independent Web design learners.

Essentially then, this small-scale project, which arose from a specific classroom need, provided the opportunity for the teacher and external expert to engage in some reflection about the use of Forum and its efficacy in promoting learning at a distance. Key questions were:

- How easy was it for students and teacher to use the system?
- How useful was it for students and teacher to have access to an external expert via an online learning system?
- What problems did the teacher experience?
- What were the benefits to students' learning through using an online facility?
- To what extent were the teacher's skills enhanced through this online external support?

FINDINGS

The Teacher

Janice, the classroom teacher, realized that, at the start, she needed to be "super-organised and . . . have a good plan." This refers to her knowledge about what the online forum's purpose was and how it should best meet both students' learning needs, and her own pedagogical purposes. She spent time in her non-teaching break (that is, in her holiday time) to create the structure of the online course as well as enter the information and instructions for the students.

When students were face-to-face in class, Janice seldom used the online forum; there was no need since she was available to answer students' queries straight away. However, when there were questions she could not answer, students could post a message for the external expert to answer, and the message was usually responded to within 24 hours. And while she was away on a trip overseas, she could still easily keep in touch with her students and guide their progress.

A key feature of the Forum was its restricted access. It was "closed" to everyone other than the students, Janice, and the external expert. Everyone who had access had an individual username and password. This restricted access made it easier for some students to feel safe enough to ask questions that exposed their lack of knowledge. This also prompted another kind of learning. Interestingly, both Janice and at least one student commented on how important it was to "get the hang" of asking accurate questions, explaining what was meant, and being "precise" with answers. In terms of learning, asking accurate questions and giving precise answers are important steps in clarifying higher order thinking.

Since Janice was also embarking on new learning at the same time as students, it was important to feel that she "wasn't alone" in this. The external expert/mentor "gave lots of moral support, encouragement and expert advice in relation to Web sites. He became a friend [at] the end of the computer." This particular aspect was critical to her ability to keep going and learning alongside students. She was, as McIsaac and Craft (2003) observe, in the position of needing to feel at ease with new materials. McIsaac and Craft suggest that, "if technology-based curricular materials are to be useful, teachers must understand how to use them, feel at ease with them, and be motivated to incorporate them into their lessons" (p. 41).

Some of the problems Janice faced, apart from the vulnerability of learning alongside students, included not having enough privileges within the school's intranet system. She often had to wait for the technician to execute moves she felt she should have been able to do for students. For instance, the system wouldn't allow her to post the final Web pages online for the national competition. This caused delays and unnecessary anxiety, since this lack of privileges was not something she had been aware of beforehand.

Another challenge for this teacher related to her unfamiliarity with assessing work online, although she felt that this was a potential area for her personal professional development. Developing her expertise to assess work online was a way, Janice believed, of making her marking more efficient, and increasing the assessment options available to her.

She also thought that an online learning system could help her to "work with students out of town who do not have the numbers to create classes and therefore have to drop the subject." While the school she works in is urban, there are nearby outlying rural schools serving farming communities that have fewer students and more restricted subject choices. This teacher's strategic thinking in this regard may help her school and others make worthwhile connections that ultimately improve students' learning choices and more effectively network teachers' expertise.

Another problem with having the students in class as well as online was that "students relied on [the teacher] too much." They "needed to get into the habit of logging in each day and reading the responses to other questions" before embarking on new work. This could have helped them more effectively learn from one another's queries and experiments. Janice also felt that this was important if they were to develop independence as learners. This aim also means that she will probably have to reconsider how she plans her program if she is to encourage students to seek answers outside the expertise of their classroom teachers. Having an online facility that allows them to seek advice from an outside expert may prove very useful in the long term.

Students

The online learning aspect of this Web page development topic was new to all students. The external expert therefore visited the classroom students to meet them all and get them logged into the system. He also showed them how to take, upload their digital photographs (which automatically accompanied each of their postings), and become familiar with how the online environment worked. This first stage, noted in Salmon's (2000) model of teaching and learning online, was recognized as a very important initial step for the students' understanding about learning online.

Some students initially resisted using the online forum, partly because it was too unfamiliar and partly because they preferred and were used to face-to-face learning. However, several students soon realized that having to write their questions and be more exact with their meanings was beneficial for them since they were forced to think carefully about their challenges and explain them clearly so that the external expert could provide effective support and advice. This meant that students' higher order thinking skills were in use. One student said that "using the online classroom has made me aware of different ways to learn and has helped [me get better at the] skills of asking questions without talking." This heightened reflective and critical thinking outcome of the project was positively serendipitous.

Many students expected online responses to be as instantaneous as responses from the teacher in the classroom. However, this only happened if the expert was online at the same time as the students. Most of the discussions were asynchronous and led to another student noting that "it is hard to have to wait for a reply when you want the answer right then and there."

Another student enjoyed the experience, saying that "it helped my learning because I am a visual person and that's how I learn, so I could see exactly what I had to do." Some students also commented on how useful it was to have notes online, since they couldn't misplace or lose them, as they did with paper handouts.

Students and Janice were particularly complimentary about the skills and help provided by the external expert. It's possible then, that their knowledge base about Web design was increased because the external expert was approachable and could make the new learning accessible and easily understood. The quality of any external expert's advice and guidance is therefore critical in supporting the learning of new skills and concepts.

One of the points raised by both students and the teacher was the 'friendliness' of the online system. This friendliness was due to students being able to 'see' who they were 'talking' to online, supplementing the face-to-face community already established in the classroom. The individual photographs being automatically attached to each person's postings supported this.

One student noted a key benefit of the online system when she said that, "if someone needed help in a subject they could just ask on the online system. Some students are too scared to ask their teachers for help [in class]." This notion of widening the pool of people to seek help from is pertinent to those interested in improving learning outcomes for secondary school students. Finding out more about students' shyness in asking questions in the classroom compared with their willingness to do so online might be a worthwhile line of further inquiry.

External Expert

The external expert noted three pertinent issues. Firstly, that the initial impetus for this project derived from the classroom teacher based on previous collaborations with the external expert and exposure to the online learning system. The prior knowledge and experience of the teacher in using this environment were therefore an important catalyst. Secondly, the preparation of the online forum was important. The external expert showed the teacher how to use it and create specific areas within the forum. The discussions that ensued once students gained access and learned how to use the online forum were initiated by both the teacher and students. This meant that the external expert responded to needs and questions rather than orchestrating the learning.

Lastly, visiting the class and making face-to-face contact with students helped the external expert establish a positive relationship with the class. This relationship was then more easily maintained online. This initial visit also meant the external expert could help students to get online using their usernames and passwords, assist students with manipulating and adding their personal photographs to their usernames, show them how to navigate the system, and explain how to post messages.

Essentially then, the role of the external expert was that of facilitation within a reciprocal learning framework. Working alongside the teacher, who was working alongside students, he adopted an approach that suited the teacher's and students' needs, responding to any learning plateau. In other words, when either the teacher or students got stuck, they sought his help by posting messages online.

Importantly, the external expert was careful throughout not to usurp the teacher's role. This careful approach has Janice seeking further help in developing her expertise, suggesting a high degree of trust and confidence in the external expert.

CONCLUSION

While this was a very small-scale teacher-initiated project, it nevertheless points to some opportunities available to extend both students' learning repertoires, and teachers' abilities to engage in on-the-job learning. An effective external expert/mentor who provides support and advice to both students and teachers is also valuable, especially if a learning collaboration between students and teachers is seen as productive for learning. The availability of the external expert to visit the class helped establish the initial connection and relationship. This may have been a significant factor for students' buy-in to the online forum. This factor is, at this stage, speculation, but is supported by Smyth and Hattam's (2004) research with Australian students who had "dropped out" (a contested term in their work) of school. One question they pursued with students related to what they saw as important at school. Students insisted that effective and positive relationships with teachers were paramount. The online forum used in this small project extended not only the connections between teacher, student and external expert, but also a collaborative and effective working relationship. The quality of the learning was also enhanced when all participants needed to be precise in their written online questions, meanings, advice and answers.

In terms of the Web design competition, the students' entries did not win. However, the results of the competition provided a benchmark for Janice so that she became more aware of the scale and demands of the competition. Her students' lack of success in the competition has not been a deterrent to further action. She is already planning ahead for the next year's competition by identifying software she wants to become proficient in. In this way, she can further support following students so that they can submit more polished competition entries.

This kind of commitment points to this teacher's intrinsic motivation for improvement, development and challenge. Her ability to take risks in her own learning openly and alongside students points to a high degree of confidence in both her relationship with students, and with the external expert. It also points to the value of having an external mentor or expert available to support teachers in secondary classrooms as they develop their professional capabilities with ICT. An online forum can easily support such learning. Ultimately, this teacher-initiated project has fostered a win-win situation for both teacher and students. The processes used by the external expert to establish and maintain relationships were pivotal to this success. And, in terms of the trial of the online learning system to support secondary classroom work, it benefited students in their learning about Web design, and increased the capacity and knowledge of the teacher at the same time.

It will be worth revisiting this teacher's use of the online learning system to measure the extent to which she has become more expert herself and is able to increase students' capacities to use such a facility effectively.

REFERENCES

Brown, M. E. (1998, November). The use of computers in New Zealand schools: A critical view. *Computers in New Zealand Schools*, *10*(3), 3-10.

Ham, V. (2001, December). Putting computers in their place–ten years on. *English in Aotearoa*, *45*, 6-13.

Ham, V., Gilmore, A., Kachelhoffer, A., Morrow, D., Moeau, P., & Wenmouth, D. (2002). *What makes for effective teacher professional development in ICT? An evaluation of the 23 ICTPD school clusters programme 1999-2001*. Wellington, NZ: Ministry of Education.

Maddux, C. D. (1997). The newest technology crisis: Teacher expertise and how to foster it. *Computers in the Schools*, *13*(3/4), 5-12.

McInerney, D., & McInerney, V. (1998). *Educational psychology: Constructing learning* (2nd ed). Sydney: Prentice Hall.

McIsaac, M. S., & Craft, E. H. (2003). Faculty development: Using distance education effectively in the classroom. *Computers in the Schools*, *20*(3), 41-49.

Rekrut, M. D. (1999, April). Using the Internet in classroom instruction: A primer for teachers. *Journal of Adolescent & Adult Literacy*, *42*(7), 546-557.

Salmon, G. (2000). *E-moderating: The key to teaching and learning online.* London: Kogan Page.

Smeets, E., & Mooij, T. (2001). Pupil-centred learning, ICT and teacher behaviour: Observations in educational practice. *British Journal of Educational Technology, 32*(4), 403-417.

Smyth, J., & Hattam, R. (2004). *'Dropping out,' drifting off, being excluded: Becoming somebody without school.* New York: Peter Lang.

Tu, C-H., & Corry, M. (2003). Building active online interaction via a collaborative learning community. *Computers in the Schools, 20*(3), 51-59.

Robert Perkins
Margaret L. McKnight

Teachers' Attitudes Toward WebQuests as a Method of Teaching

SUMMARY. One of the latest uses of technology gaining popular status in education is the WebQuest, a process that involves students using the World Wide Web to solve a problem. The goals of this project are to: (a) determine if teachers are using WebQuests in their classrooms; (b) ascertain whether teachers feel WebQuests are effective for teaching students; (c) determine some of the problems associated with using WebQuests; and (d) discover the relationship between teachers' comfort level using WebQuests and the degree to which they are integrating WebQuests into classroom curriculum, by using the Stages of Concern Questionnaire. *[Article copies available for a fee from The Haworth Document Delivery Service: 1-800-HAWORTH. E-mail address: <docdelivery@ haworthpress.com> Website: <http://www.HaworthPress.com> © 2005 by The Haworth Press, Inc. All rights reserved.]*

KEYWORDS. WebQuests, WWW, computers in education, Stages of Concern

ROBERT PERKINS is Department Chair, Educational Foundations, Secondary and Special Education (EDFS), School of Education, College of Charleston, Charleston, SC 29424 (E-mail: perkinsr@cofc.edu).
MARGARET L. MCKNIGHT is Associate Director of the Barrier Island Environmental Education Center, Johns Island, SC 29455 (E-mail: mcknightmeg@hotmail.com).

[Haworth co-indexing entry note]: "Teachers' Attitudes Toward WebQuests as a Method of Teaching." Perkins, Robert, and Margaret L. McKnight. Co-published simultaneously in *Computers in the Schools* (The Haworth Press, Inc.) Vol. 22, No. 1/2, 2005, pp. 123-133; and: *Internet Applications of Type II Uses of Technology in Education* (ed: Cleborne D. Maddux, and D. LaMont Johnson) The Haworth Press, Inc., 2005, pp. 123-133. Single or multiple copies of this article are available for a fee from The Haworth Document Delivery Service [1-800-HAWORTH, 9:00 a.m. - 5:00 p.m. (EST). E-mail address: docdelivery@haworthpress.com].

Available online at http://www.haworthpress.com/web/CITS
© 2005 by The Haworth Press, Inc. All rights reserved.
Digital Object Identifier: 10.1300/J025v22n01_11

Many useful ideas integrating computer use in classrooms have been proposed since personal computers first appeared in classrooms. Some of these proposed uses have come and gone, while others are still used today. Because of the expenses associated with computers and Internet access and the recent demand for accountability, educators should seriously look at the validity of these uses before implementing them into the classroom curricula. One of the latest implementations to gain popular status is the WebQuest, which involves having students access the Web to complete a task or solve a problem. The WebQuest is created by determining a problem to be solved, defining the steps involved in solving the problem, and providing resources for students to use. In the process of problem solving, students learn skills in an interactive, involved manner rather than in isolation.

REVIEW OF THE LITERATURE

WebQuest, a term coined by Dodge and March (Dodge, 2001), is one of the latest practices in classroom use of the Internet and World Wide Web. Dodge stated, "A WebQuest is an inquiry-oriented activity in which some or all of the information that learners interact with comes from resources on the Internet, optionally supplemented with videoconferencing" (2001, para. 2). According to Dodge's Web site at San Diego State University, the following are critical attributes of a WebQuest: an introduction, task, information sources, guidance on how to organize the information acquired and a conclusion that brings closure to the quest (Dodge, 1997, para. 5).

"WebQuests challenge student intellectual and academic ability rather than Web searching skills" (Vidoni & Maddux, 2002, p. 104). Vidoni and Maddux use Weinstein's critical thinking framework to demonstrate how WebQuests foster critical thinking. Students have to evaluate the sites that are used for useful information while eliminating misinformation. This helps students develop their critical thinking skills. Next, students use primary sources of information such as local, state, and national laws, and community service agencies. WebQuests are nonlinear and interdisciplinary requiring students to recognize the many issues that they deal with within the WebQuests. Criteria, or structures such as laws, standards, and principles are filtered by students as they use primary sources to form their own opinions. Lastly, students have access to many different viewpoints during the WebQuest, something that was not as available before the existence of the Internet.

There is concern with students having free access to the Internet. WebQuests address that concern (Summerville, 2000; Yoder, 1999). There are many controversial sites on the Internet. WebQuests do not require students to use search engines, and this reduces the chance that students will access inappropriate material (Vidoni & Maddux, 2002). WebQuests are useful because they include links only to the applicable online resources, thus providing an efficient and focused lesson.

It is necessary to incorporate instructional strategies that avoid the learner losing direction in the WebQuest (Lin & Hsieh, 2001). It is important to approach the learner control of lessons very cautiously (Lin & Hsieh) as too much control may result in learner confusion. There should also be a way for students to find their way back to an index or the original Web site.

Summerville (2000) states that teachers must also be aware of other potential problems with WebQuests. It is possible that students may still access inappropriate sites, accidentally or on purpose. Developing WebQuests also takes time, and the amount depends on the teachers' skills and the length of time students are expected to spend completing the WebQuest. Finally, dead links, which are links that worked previously but do not at the time the WebQuest is undertaken, can be a serious problem. Since the Web is constantly changing, teachers must check their WebQuest links before students attempt to use them.

Additional problems integrating WebQuests were reported by Dutt-Doner, Wilmer, Stevens, and Hartmann (2000). A WebQuest was used to integrate technology into their curriculum; focus the learners' time on using information rather than finding it; and taking students to a more in-depth level of analysis, synthesis, and evaluation of learning. Problems encountered in their project included: Students obtained inaccurate information, teachers tried to manage too many students on computers at one time, and first-time WebQuesters experienced logistical problems.

METHODOLOGY

Design

A survey was developed that incorporated demographic information, knowledge of and experience with implementing WebQuests, and an adapted Stages of Concern Questionnaire (SoCQ). The Stages of Concern Questionnaire is a survey that measures individuals' concern over implementing an innovation, in this case WebQuests. This survey was created for online use. The results of the Stages of Concern Questionnaire were compared to the demographic information to determine relationships.

Participants

Potential subjects for this survey were 882 participants in a state instructional technology conference who were primarily K-12 teachers, but also included higher education faculty, district-level administrators, and technology vendors. Since this population was likely to be familiar with innovative instructional technology (by virtue of choosing to attend the conference), we felt they could provide useful data. One hundred thirty-nine participants completed the survey; however, the data from six were not incorporated since they did not complete the SoCQ. The low return rate (15%) can be explained by the numerous e-mails we received from conference participants stating that, since they did not use WebQuests, they did not participate in the survey.

Materials

Our survey included the following demographic-related questions: Do you have a computer at home? Do you have a computer in the classroom? Do you have more than one computer in the classroom? Do you have access to a computer lab? Do you use the Web for your own purposes? Do you have students develop their own Web pages? Do you use WebQuests in your classroom? Do you create WebQuests for your students? What is your age? gender? degree? or, school type (rural, suburban, urban)? We included a modified version of the Stages of Concern Questionnaire that was made available on the survey Web site. Conference participants were e-mailed the address where the survey was located and asked to complete it.

The Stages of Concern Questionnaire (SoCQ) was developed to measure concerns related to innovations (Hall, George, & Rutherford, 1977). "To be concerned means to be in a mentally aroused state about something. The intensity of the arousal will depend on the person's past experiences and associations with the subject of the arousal" (Hall et al., p. 5). Hall et al. state that the *perception* stimulates concern, not the reality. Certain concerns are more intense than others, which places the respondent at a particular stage.

Hall et al. (1977) use the following stages in their questionnaire:

0 Awareness: Little concern about or involvement with the innovation.

1 Informational: A general awareness of the innovation and interest in learning more detail about it.

2 Personal: Individual is uncertain about the demands of the innovation, her/his inadequacy to meet those demands, and her/his role with the innovation.

3 Management: Attention is focused on the processes and tasks of using the innovation and the best use of information and resources.

4 Consequence: Attention focuses on impact of the innovation on students.

5 Collaboration: The focus is on coordination and cooperation with others.

6 Refocusing: The focus is on exploration of more universal benefits from the innovation. (Hall et al., p. 7)

Stages of Concern Questionnaire

The questionnaire consisted of 35 questions. Each stage is represented by combining the results of five questions. Statements in our survey included: I am concerned about people's attitudes toward WebQuests; I now know of several approaches for how I might go about using WebQuests; I don't even know what a WebQuest is; I am concerned about not having enough time to learn about WebQuests so that I can use them effectively; and, I would like to help other people use WebQuests. Participants responded to a seven-point Likert scale from: Not True of Me Now (0-1), Somewhat True of Me Now (2-5), and Very True of Me Now (6-7).

SoCQ results can be statistically compared by demographic category. Hall et al. (1977) suggest using raw data for any analysis, but reporting percentiles for graphic displays. They also provide graphs of typical results–novices (higher concerns at the earlier stages) to experts (higher at the later stages).

The SoCQ has been used to measure a variety of innovations related to educational technology. Hope (1997) administered the SoCQ to teachers to understand their emotional responses to microcomputer technology. Anderson and Reed (1998) used the SoCQ to measure changes in concern after instruction in an Internet course.

Results

An ANOVA was done to determine if there were differences in SoCQ scores by various demographic categories. Comparing the SoCQ scores of teachers who had used WebQuests with those who had not with the following demographic data showed no statistical difference: having a computer at home; having a computer in the classroom; having more than one computer in the classroom; having access to a computer lab; using the Web for their own purposes; having students develop their own Web pages; the teacher's age, gender or degree, and school type (rural, suburban, urban).

Using the Stages of Concern Questionnaire, we noted that teachers who had used WebQuests were lower at the Awareness, Informational, Personal, and Management stages than those who had not used WebQuests but were higher at the Consequence, Collaboration, and Refocusing stages (see Table 1). The graphs are reported in percentiles and tables of the statistical analysis were conducted on raw data (per the suggestion of Hall et al., 1977).

Hall et al. (1977) also provided samples of typical graphs of data showing that nonusers of an innovation are typically higher at the early stages based on their novice knowledge. Figure 1 shows that nonusers of WebQuests followed that pattern. Their concerns were highest at the Awareness, Informational, Personal, and Management stages. Those who had used WebQuests also followed a typical pattern: low in the early stages but high for Consequence, Collaboration, and Refocusing. All stages were significantly different between the two groups.

Teachers who had created WebQuests were lower at the Awareness, Informational, Personal, and Management stages of the SoCQ than those who had not created WebQuests, but were higher at the Consequence, Collaboration, and Refocusing stages than those who had not

TABLE 1. Teachers Who Had Used WebQuests vs. Those Who Had Not

Stage	Mean		Standard Deviation		$F(1, 131)$	p
	Had not used WebQuests ($n = 69$)	Had used WebQuests ($n = 64$)	Had not used WebQuests	Had used WebQuests		
Awareness	9.90	3.30	6.63	5.02	41.43	.0001
Informational	19.48	14.56	10.27	7.79	9.57	.0024
Personal	14.86	9.67	8.59	7.13	14.21	.0002
Management	9.41	6.20	6.99	5.34	8.71	.0037
Consequence	13.97	19.03	10.09	9.28	9.02	.0032
Collaboration	18.03	26.75	10.98	7.50	28.16	.0001
Refocusing	15.30	22.30	9.76	7.78	20.67	.0001

FIGURE 1. Stages of Concern plotted for those who had and had not used WebQuests.

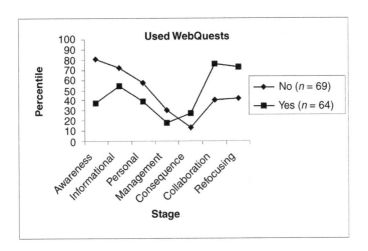

created WebQuests (see Table 2). Figure 2 shows the percentiles graphically. Again, all stages were significantly different.

Our survey also contained open-ended questions. The first question was: What is the best thing about WebQuests? A few specific themes became apparent in the replies. First, the most common comment revolved around the structured nature of WebQuests because students are presented with links to useful information. As long as WebQuests are well-constructed, student time is used efficiently: All useless information has been weeded out.

Many comments revolved around the interactive nature of WebQuests. Students are involved in the process as they participate in the lesson. They are constantly interacting because they must research the WebQuest topic. One respondent commented that WebQuests are a collaborative activity. As a result, students are less likely to be bored with the learning process. They learn as they "play" on the Internet. This WebQuest interaction is motivating for students. They enjoy the activities involved in solving the WebQuests.

The next concept addressed was the nature of the student involvement in the WebQuest and how learners of differing abilities can be involved. Students can set the pace of their involvement in the WebQuest.

TABLE 2. Teachers Who Had Created WebQuests vs. Those Who Had Not

Stage	Mean		Standard Deviation		$F(1, 131)$	p
	Had not created WebQuests ($n = 69$)	Had created WebQuests ($n = 64$)	Had not created WebQuests	Had created WebQuests		
Awareness	9.44	3.80	6.79	5.39	27.83	.0001
Informational	20.03	13.97	9.97	7.79	15.11	.0002
Personal	15.01	9.50	8.51	7.11	16.32	.0001
Management	9.68	5.91	7.06	5.04	12.43	.0006
Consequence	13.91	19.09	10.02	9.33	9.49	.0025
Collaboration	18.42	26.33	11.17	7.68	22.30	.0001
Refocusing	15.54	22.05	9.83	7.90	17.55	.0001

FIGURE 2. Stages of Concern plotted for those who had and had not created WebQuests.

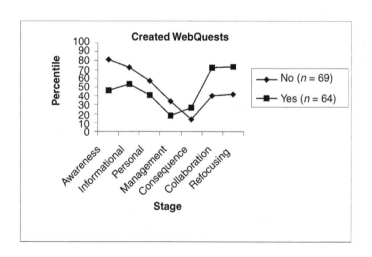

The activity also can tap each student's strengths. The many possible learning styles can also be addressed. Using the Internet provides practice in using auditory, visual, reading, thinking and problem-solving skills. While some students may need assistance from their peers, others can move at a faster pace.

Lastly, respondents commented that WebQuests are an effective way to have their students involved with technology. Web resources are far more numerous than those available through other media. WebQuests allow both teachers and students to learn by a method that is more effective, engaging, and meaningful. One teacher even commented that he/she had students create the WebQuests.

Responses to the question "What is the worst thing about WebQuests in the classroom?" also revolved around a few main themes. Twelve people commented that facilities were a problem. Others commented that computer resources were insufficient and did not allow for all students to have use of a computer. The student-computer ratio, they felt, made it difficult to use WebQuests effectively.

The second most prevalent negative comment concerned the time involved. One problem was that WebQuests could not be completed in the allotted time, and they questioned whether the time involved was worth the educational payoff. Time also was a concern for five teachers who stated that it is very time consuming to create a quality WebQuest.

Six teachers were concerned with technology issues: computers crashing, faulty connections, and links that no longer worked. Since access to the Internet and the Web is integral in making WebQuests a success, any difficulty accessing the Web would make the lesson impossible to complete.

Students who do not have basic keyboarding skills had difficulty. Lack of experience maneuvering within the Web or lack of understanding of browsers may be two factors affecting student ability to use WebQuests effectively. Another teacher commented that WebQuests are often too difficult. One teacher commented that students do not like them because the answers are readily apparent. Another issue is finding Web sites at the appropriate readability level.

Creating a high-quality WebQuest requires an understanding of the elements of a good WebQuest, and also specific skills. Many teachers do not know how to create Web pages, and one teacher suggested starting on a smaller scale by using a Web site like TrackStar. One teacher complained about Netscape Composer as a Web page editor.

The last negative statement regarding WebQuests was related to the quality of available WebQuests. One teacher commented that "I have to say far and few between are acceptable. There are too many errors in most WebQuests and many are not very well prepared."

The next question in the survey asked those who had used a Web-Quest in their classroom to describe the experience. Forty-one of 66 respondents said they had used WebQuests in the classroom and described this as a positive experience. Comments ranged from "It went well" to "It worked very well and was thoroughly enjoyed by all the students involved." These are some of the specific comments made:

- WebQuests provide students with the necessary structure to complete a complex task independently. They provide opportunities for students to practice higher order thinking skills and they provide students with the opportunity to put the skills into practice.
- WebQuests allow the students to become more responsible for their education.
- Wonderful! The students love the cooperative nature of the WebQuest and it allowed each student to go as far as he/she could.

CONCLUSIONS

Demographic information did not reveal any surprises. Those who had developed and used Web pages with their students were more likely to use or develop WebQuests. Interestingly, access to a computer at home, in the classroom, or in a lab was not a factor. The teachers' age, gender, and degree, as well as school type, were also not factors. Teachers with all characteristics in all kinds of schools were equally likely to use or create WebQuests.

The Stages of Concern Questionnaire results were exactly as expected. In fact, plots for both novice users and creators of WebQuests were what Hall et al. (1977) had suggested a typical novice plot would look like. The concerns of novices are more focused on trying to learn about WebQuests and how using WebQuests will affect the teacher directly as opposed to experienced users and developers, who are trying to see what else they can do with the innovation.

The open-ended questions also provided no new revelations to those who have created or used WebQuests. They are an excellent educational innovation when used correctly. They can keep students focused on the Web sites that provide information relative to the task at hand. But, as noted by the teachers, they are not without problems. The usual technological issues of equipment reliability, student-computer ratio, and student skills are relevant factors.

It was encouraging to see all the positive comments about Web-Quests. When properly created and used, they provide an interesting way for students to attack real problems in a focused way. Probably the most important factor was the quality of the WebQuests. As with other things that are found on the Web, there are both good and bad WebQuests. All WebQuests will not work for all classrooms. As with other teaching strategies, they do not work for all students. Teachers need to preview the WebQuests they find and double-check them too before having the students use them.

Technology is always touted as being a panacea for ills in education. Research into effective uses of technology is important to justify its continued use. Since WebQuests are a new implementation of technology, a knowledge base surrounding effectiveness needs to be developed. Schools in many states are accountability driven based on performance testing; and some schools are seeing a backlash against technology and a desire for a back-to-basics movement to raise test scores. Teachers feel that technology is providing the knowledge in an interesting fashion to students; its use should be continued and even encouraged.

REFERENCES

Anderson, D. K., & Reed, W. M. (1998). The effects of Internet instruction, prior computer experience, and learning style on teachers' Internet attitudes and knowledge. *Journal of Educational Computing Research, 19*(3), 227-246.

Dodge, B. (1997). *Some thoughts about WebQuests.* Retrieved June 9, 2004, from the San Diego State University College of Education Web site: http://edWeb. sdsu.edu/courses/edtec596/about_WebQuests.html.

Dodge, B. (2004). *Site overview.* Retrieved June 9, 2004, from the WebQuest page: http://Webquest.sdsu.edu/overview.htm.

Dutt-Doner, K., Wilmer, M., Stevens, C., & Hartmann, L. (2000). Actively engaging learners in interdisciplinary curriculum through the integration of technology. *Computer in the Schools, 16*(3/4), 151-166.

Hall, G. E., George, A. A., & Rutherford, W. L. (1977). *Measuring stages of concern about the innovation: A manual for use of the SoC Questionnaire.* (Eric Reproduction Service No. ED 147 342).

Hope, W. C. (1997). Resolving teachers' concerns about microcomputer technology. *Computers in the Schools, 13*(3/4), 147-160.

Summerville, J. (2000). WebQuests. *TechTrends, 44*(2), 31-35.

Vidoni, K. L., & Maddux, C. D. (2002). WebQuests: Can they be used to improve critical thinking skills in students? *Computers in the Schools, 19*(1/2), 101-117.

Yoder, M. B. (1999). The student WebQuest: A productive and thought-provoking use of the Internet. *Learning and Leading with Technology, 26*(7), 6-9.

Michelle P. Orme
Eula Ewing Monroe

The Nature of Discourse as Students Collaborate on a Mathematics WebQuest

SUMMARY. Students were audiotaped while working in teams on a WebQuest. Although gender-segregated, each team included both fifth- and sixth-graders. Interactions from two tasks were analyzed according to categories (exploratory, cumulative, disputational, tutorial) defined by the Spoken Language and New Technology (SLANT) project (e.g., Wegerif & Scrimshaw, 1997) and were coded as either mathematical or task-procedural. Findings emerged related to three major themes: task, gender, and power. For one task, student discourse was largely mathematical, with cumulative and tutorial discourse patterns predominant; for the other task, interactions were primarily task-procedural and followed mostly cumulative and disputational patterns. Exploratory discourse, considered to be the most educationally useful (Fisher, 1997), occurred during both tasks. Largely, girls' interactions were characterized by cooperation and boys' interactions by disputations. Disputations

MICHELLE P. ORME is a former graduate student, Department of Teacher Education, Brigham Young University, Provo, UT 84602 (E-mail: jeffryrorme@juno.com).
EULA EWING MONROE is Professor, Mathematics Education, Department of Teacher Education, Brigham Young University, Provo, UT 84602 (E-mail: Eula_Monroe@byu.edu).
The authors would like to thank Annela Teemant of Brigham Young University who guided the research design for this project, and Robin Watson, who assisted with editing.

[Haworth co-indexing entry note]: "The Nature of Discourse as Students Collaborate on a Mathematics WebQuest." Orme, Michelle P., and Eula Ewing Monroe. Co-published simultaneously in *Computers in the Schools* (The Haworth Press, Inc.) Vol. 22, No. 1/2, 2005, pp. 135-146; and: *Internet Applications of Type II Uses of Technology in Education* (ed: Cleborne D. Maddux, and D. LaMont Johnson) The Haworth Press, Inc., 2005, pp. 135-146. Single or multiple copies of this article are available for a fee from The Haworth Document Delivery Service [1-800-HAWORTH, 9:00 a.m. - 5:00 p.m. (EST). E-mail address: docdelivery@haworthpress.com].

Available online at http://www.haworthpress.com/web/CITS
© 2005 by The Haworth Press, Inc. All rights reserved.
Digital Object Identifier: 10.1300/J025v22n01_12

also occurred between team members of differing grade levels regarding how power was held and used. *[Article copies available for a fee from The Haworth Document Delivery Service: 1-800-HAWORTH. E-mail address: <docdelivery@haworthpress.com> Website: <http://www.HaworthPress.com> © 2005 by The Haworth Press, Inc. All rights reserved.]*

KEYWORDS. WebQuests, technology, discourse, elementary mathematics, technology, collaborative learning, cumulative patterns, disputational patterns

"Technologies are tools for supporting and amplifying human activity. Technologies shape the way people act and think" (Jonassen, Hernandez-Serrano, & Choi, 2000, p. 113). Advocates for using technology in education believe that learners can do more with the assistance of technology than they might do without it. They also believe that learning with technology is more likely to be "assimilated" (Jonassen et al., 2000, p. 113) into the cognitive structures of the brain than learning without the use of technology.

In *Principles and Standards for School Mathematics* (National Council of Teachers of Mathematics [NCTM], 2000), technology was identified as one of six basic principles upon which mathematics instruction should be based. According to NCTM, "Technology is essential in teaching and learning mathematics; it influences the mathematics that is taught and enhances students' learning" (p. 24). NCTM proposes that technology can foster conceptual understandings by providing visual representations and quick and accurate computations while supporting student investigation. Through the use of technology, students can solve problems and engage in meaningful activities that otherwise may be beyond their reach.

Mathematical communication has been recognized as a central process in helping students develop and refine their conceptual understandings (NCTM, 1991, 2000). Students need ample opportunity for discourse during mathematics study to enable them to "organize and consolidate their mathematical thinking" and to "communicate their mathematical thinking coherently and clearly" (NCTM, 2000, pp. 60-61). Within the context of a well-designed task, the appropriate use of technology can provide opportunities for meaningful discourse while offering exciting possibilities for teaching and learning unheard of a decade ago.

One such possibility is the WebQuest. A WebQuest is "an inquiry-oriented activity in which some or all of the information that learners interact with comes from resources on the Internet" (Dodge, 1997, May 5, "Definitions," para. 1). Designed by Bernie Dodge and Tom March at San Diego State University in early 1995, WebQuests are receiving increased attention from educators (Dodge, 2001, October 27). WebQuest advocates claim that these computer-based tasks can integrate the Internet safely into the classroom while supporting student efforts to think analytically. Web sites are specified in advance, preventing "accidental" viewing of inappropriate material. In well-designed WebQuests, students have a relevant, compelling task that can be accomplished only by searching for and applying information found on the specified Web pages. Student efforts are scaffolded throughout the WebQuest with specific directions on how to proceed. The tasks require high levels of thinking as students construct meanings and, ideally, work collaboratively to accomplish the tasks.

Despite claims in the literature that WebQuests can promote meaningful student interactions (e.g., Dodge, 2001), no descriptions of such interactions were located. The purpose of this study was to describe the nature of student oral discourse while engaging in a WebQuest.

METHOD

Participants

A multiage class of 24 students, 9 fifth-graders and 15 sixth-graders, from a small city in the intermountain West participated in this study. The group included 9 females and 15 males, all fluent English speakers. The elementary school these students attend serves a predominantly Caucasian student body in the low- to middle-income ranges.

The WebQuest

The WebQuest selected, "A Creative Encounter of the Numerical Kind" (Gabbard, n.d.), designed to help middle school students deepen their understanding of the base-ten numeration system, specifies that participants are to work in groups, or teams, of three. The WebQuest comprises five major tasks:

1. Activating prior knowledge by completing the K and W portions of a K-W-L chart ("What We **K**now," "What We **W**ant to Learn," and "What We Learned" [Ogle, 1986]). The L segment of the chart was completed in a debriefing session at the end of the WebQuest.
2. Conducting independent online research about historical numeration systems, use of an abacus, and the current base-ten system; each team member being assigned specific Web sites to visit.
3. Teaching other members of the team what he or she learned during independent research.
4. As a group, creating a way of writing numbers in base four for the Zony tribe, an alien species whose members have two fingers on each hand. (In this study this task is labeled "creating a unique number system.")
5. Collaboratively preparing and presenting a final project that shares the new number system. (In this study this task is labeled "creating a visual aid.")

This WebQuest was found on San Diego State University's Web-Quest Page, in the "Matrix of Examples" (Dodge, 2002, February 18). The exemplars on the "Matrix" page were chosen by WebQuest creator Dodge (B. Dodge, personal communication, January 28, 2002) as meeting criteria similar to those found in the "Rubric for Evaluating WebQuests" (Bellofatto, Bohl, Casey, Krill, & Dodge, 2001, June 19). When the researcher evaluated "A Creative Encounter of the Numerical Kind" (Gabbard, n.d.) using the Bellofatto et al. rubric, the WebQuest scored 44.2 points of a possible 50. A university faculty member with expertise in both technology and mathematics education also evaluated the WebQuest according to the same rubric, scoring it at 45 points.

Procedure

Administering the WebQuest. The researcher administered the WebQuest to the subjects during the last hour of the school day for 10 sessions over a three-week period. During each session, audio recorders were placed with two different groups to record interactions, with each group recorded at least twice and two groups recorded three times. Transcriptions of these recordings, along with notes made by the researcher after each teaching session, served as primary data sources for this study.

With the guidance of the regular classroom teacher, the researcher assigned students to groups of three, with both fifth- and sixth-graders in each group. Girls and boys were assigned to separate groups to eliminate the potential for inequality in discourse that might occur in a mixed-gender group (e.g., Swann, 1997).

During most of each WebQuest period, students collaborated in working on the tasks defined within the WebQuest; the researcher circulated, answering questions regarding procedures and providing prompts to encourage student thinking. The researcher addressed student needs that emerged–making group decisions, making mathematical connections, managing time, brainstorming, grouping and counting in base four, etc.–through whole-group discussion. Students were provided explicit instruction on how to bookmark the WebQuest, navigate the Internet, help an off-task partner, and complete a complicated portion of the visual aid. During the last five minutes of most sessions, students were asked to engage in group processing (e.g., Johnson & Johnson, n.d.). During this time they evaluated their progress and discussed how to improve their group skills, responding orally to these questions: (a) What did we do well? (b) What do we need to do next time to improve?

Adaptations to the WebQuest. In implementing the WebQuest, several adaptations were made:

1. To help students become more comfortable with the WebQuest and with their group assignments, the researcher asked the class to complete the first assignment, activating prior knowledge, in teams instead of individually.
2. Because few students had e-mail accounts, students printed their research guides and completed them by hand, rather than completing them on the computer and submitting them by e-mail.
3. The Web browser did not support an applet designed to allow students to manipulate an online abacus. Instead, students used beans and cups as manipulatives for counting and grouping in base four.
4. Because of time constraints, students wrote the numerals from 1 to 30 rather than to 70 in their new number systems.

Computer Considerations. The students' regular instruction included a 30-minute computer lab period each week; however, Internet instruction received little emphasis. The lab was equipped with 28 Internet-active iMac computers, built-in CD-ROM drives, and printers; during the study, the lab was available for the sessions, with additional Internet access via the classroom computer. To complete the WebQuest, each team of students used Netscape Communicator and WordPerfect. One team also used the spreadsheet application of AppleWorks to organize and present the number system developed.

Data Analysis

In order to describe the nature of students' discourse during a WebQuest, categories of oral discourse were used to analyze transcribed student conversations. The researcher used exploratory, cumulative, disputational, and tutorial categories as defined by SLANT (e.g., Fisher, 1997; Scrimshaw & Perkins, 1997; Wegerif & Mercer, 1997) and summarized in Table 1.

Of the four categories of discourse, exploratory discourse is believed to be the most educationally useful when working in collaborative projects with computers (Fisher, 1997). It allows "different voices to inter-animate each other in a way which not only constructs shared knowledge but also critically assesses the quality of that knowledge" (Wegerif & Mercer, 1997, p. 59). Thus exploratory discourse in collaborative learning environments can encourage opposition between ideas, not people, with the ideas that are judged best by the group becoming dominant. The researcher was particularly interested in whether stu-

TABLE 1. Patterns of Classroom Discourse Used in Coding Data

Category	Description
Exploratory	Discussion without animosity: posing of hypotheses, counterhypotheses with justifications. Participants select one of the suggestions or modify a suggestion. Teammates are equal.
Cumulative	Agreement: elaborations, confirmations, and repetitions build on the initiating statement. No real difference of opinions; ideas are accepted without debate. Teammates are mostly equal.
Disputational	Disagreement: following an initiating hypothesis or suggestion, a counterhypothesis or rejection of initiating hypothesis is offered by teammate. Not progressing toward completing task; no resolution, or resolution requiring a group member to "lose face."
Tutorial	Team members go from an equal to an unequal relationship. One member becomes tutor; tutee(s) are willing to be taught.

Note. The term *hypothesis* refers to students' ideas or suggestions offered in a discussion.

dents' collaborative conversation during the WebQuest would include exploratory discourse.

The transcriptions were examined initially to determine which tasks produced the most collaborative conversation. The framework for evaluating student oral discourse for indications of collaboration was provided by Tiessen and Ward (1997). Tiessen and Ward assert that for collaboration to occur, students must engage in communication and cooperation while sharing the same work area to create some original item. The segments of transcribed data determined to be most collaborative occurred during these tasks: "creating a unique number system" and "creating a visual aid." Transcripts of hour-long tapes from a group of boys and a group of girls were selected for each of these collaborative activities, for a total of four transcripts from four different groups.

Transcripts were analyzed for patterns of discourse according to the SLANT categories (see Table 1), and boundaries of interactions were marked. The categories of discourse that emerged during coding determined these boundaries. For example, exploratory and disputational interactions frequently begin with an initiating statement and have some type of resolution at the end. However, cumulative and tutorial interactions "end" when the discourse shifts to a different pattern or topic. For any interaction containing two or more categories of discourse–e.g., a cumulative interaction interrupted briefly by a disputational interchange–the data were coded according to the category that fit the majority of the interaction. A research assistant also coded the interactions according to the SLANT categories. When the results of the two codings were compared, the agreement rate was 93%.

Interactions were also coded as mathematical or task/procedural. Discourse was labeled mathematical when students discussed mathematical ideas important to completing the WebQuest (e.g., place value). The task-procedural label was applied when students discussed a detail related to the WebQuest, but not related to the mathematical ideas under study.

FINDINGS

The tasks "creating a unique number system" and "creating a visual aid" were selected for in-depth analysis because they elicited the most collaborative discourse. The content and pattern of student conversation within the four teams under study (one male team, one female team for each of the two most collaborative tasks) varied according to the task analyzed. During analysis, findings emerged related to three major themes: task, gender, and power.

Task

The nature of discourse differed across the two tasks under study. "Creating a unique number system," largely involving mathematical ideas, generated discourse that was primarily either cumulative or tutorial. Students discussed a wide range of mathematical concepts and procedures related to the task (e.g., what symbols to use while creating a unique number system, how to count in base four, how numbers higher than four were to be named in their unique number system). In contrast, "creating a visual aid" was primarily procedural for the students (e.g., interpreting instructions related to the task, how to organize the visual aid, which team member would do the writing, with both males and females involved in cumulative interactions). However, males were involved in disputational interactions more frequently than in any of the other discourse categories during "creating a visual aid." See Table 2 for a summary of the types of interactions produced during these two tasks.

TABLE 2. Types of Interactions Produced During Two Most Collaborative Tasks

			SLANT categories			
Gender	Mathematical interactions	Task-procedural interactions	Exploratory	Cumulative	Disputational	Tutorial
Creating a unique number system						
Boys	13	5	3	9	3	3
Girls	4	1	0	1	1	3
Total	17	6	3	10	4	6
Completing a visual aid						
Boys	4	38	2	15	23	4
Girls	3	7	4	6	0	2
Total	7	45	6	21	23	6

Note: Both teams completing the visual aid had 2 interactions each that were classified as neither mathematical nor task-procedural.

Both tasks under study allowed for exploratory discourse about mathematical ideas, presenting opportunities for participants to reason, discuss, analyze, and connect mathematics concepts. The first task, "creating a unique number system," elicited exploratory discourse patterns among the boys. These discussions are summarized as follows: (a) naming higher order numbers in base four (related to place value), and (b) discussing what was easier to remember in relation to names they selected for symbols. For girls, the task "creating a visual aid" elicited exploratory discourse regarding (a) writing in base four with unique symbols, and (b) using exponents.

Gender

The nature of discourse for the teams analyzed also differed depending on the gender of the speakers. In exploratory interactions, girls often used phrases that softened their hypotheses (e.g., "I think we should . . . ," "We could do . . . ," "Unless you want . . ."). In tutorial interactions, girls being tutored asked questions about what they did not understand and repeated what they heard and or saw to check for understanding. Across discourse categories, girls also had frequent utterances of "okay," indicating agreement or affirmation. They sometimes sought confirmation before performing a task.

Boys had a tendency to give commands in cumulative, disputational, and exploratory discourse. In the following excerpt from a boys' exploratory interaction, note the two commands in this short interchange.

Request:	Can somebody else do this now?
Command:	Uh, you write up to a point and then I'll do like the 10 times 10 and stuff.
Statement:	That's easy.
Statement, with a "no":	No, it's not.
Command:	I already did four now, [name of other student], you do the other three.
Statement:	It should probably look the same.

In cumulative interactions, boys displayed few repetitions, but contributed by offering elaborations. Boys had frequent disputational interactions. In tutorial interactions, boy tutors directed the discourse; boy tutees were sometimes passive.

Power

The discourse reflected different distributions of power within the groups under study. Sixth-graders in one team held power by controlling the task at hand and by choosing which suggestions and resolutions were accepted. Fifth-graders in another team resisted sixth-grade control by ignoring or arguing with the sixth-grader who took charge. One girls' team had equality, with a team leader within the group who directed but did not dominate group work.

DISCUSSION

The need for students to engage in rich discourse about mathematical ideas is widely expressed in the mathematics education literature (NCTM, 2000). The research available, albeit limited in quantity and scope, indicates that WebQuests with embedded concepts (e.g., "A Creative Encounter of the Numerical Kind" [Gabbard, n.d.]) may be useful for generating such discussions. On the other hand, WebQuests that focus heavily on a specific product or procedure are likely to evoke less mathematical discourse. The findings of this study support the need for WebQuests to involve conceptually significant tasks to elicit exploratory discourse about important mathematics concepts and procedures, the kind of discourse that appears most likely to lead to conceptual development (Fisher, 1997; NCTM, 2000). However, in this study, even a task that required some attention to procedures produced exploratory discourse regarding concepts. Although the tasks analyzed varied in level of conceptual demand, both elicited reasoning and discussion of important mathematical ideas.

For the multiage classroom under study, power appeared to be associated with grade levels within students' assigned teams as well as gender of team members. Power emerged as a factor affecting the nature of student discourse. This finding raises more questions than it answers. Regardless of how students are assigned to groups, teachers need to give attention to scaffolding students' collaborative efforts. Interpersonal and small group skills must be taught in order for cooperative ventures to succeed (e.g., Johnson & Johnson, n.d.). Watson (1997a) developed an intervention program focusing specifically on teaching cooperative skills to students in a computer-based learning environment. Her program improved the quality of interactions between boys and girls working with computers, thus demonstrating a successful method for reducing gender bias in computer environments.

The study reported in this paper was an introductory effort to describe the nature of student discourse during work on WebQuests; many unanswered questions remain. Some unresolved issues that emerged during this study include the following:

1. Although student discourse varied with the assigned tasks, little is known about the nature of WebQuest tasks that best evoke conceptually relevant mathematical discourse and how these tasks should interrelate in the WebQuest experience.
2. Whether genders are mixed or segregated, communication patterns related to gender emerge (Lee, 1993; Swann, 1997; Watson, 1997b). Future research needs to examine discourse influenced by grouping boys and girls heterogeneously during WebQuests.
3. Research is needed on the nature of power relationships among team members during WebQuests in order to learn how to achieve the equality within groups that promotes conceptually relevant discourse.

With the likelihood that WebQuests will become increasingly familiar as a teaching strategy, the issue of how best to design and use them to meet the goals of mathematics instruction is a high priority.

REFERENCES

Bellofatto, L., Bohl, N., Casey, M., Krill, M., & Dodge, B. (2001, June 19). *A rubric for evaluating WebQuests*. Retrieved September 25, 2001, from San Diego State University, Educational Technology Department, The WebQuest Page: http://webquest.sdsu.edu/webquestrubric.html

Dodge, B. (1997, May 5). *Some thoughts about WebQuests*. Retrieved September 20, 2001, from San Diego State University, Educational Technology Department, The WebQuest Page: http://edweb.sdsu.edu/courses/edtec596/about_webquests.html

Dodge, B. (2001). FOCUS: Five rules for writing a great WebQuest [Electronic version]. *Learning and Leading with Technology, 28*(8), 6-9, 58.

Dodge, B. (2001, October 27). *Site overview*. Retrieved February 20, 2002, from San Diego State University, Educational Technology Department, The WebQuest Page: http://webquest.sdsu.edu/overview.htm

Dodge, B. (2002, February 18). *Matrix of examples*. Retrieved February 20, 2002, from San Diego State University, Educational Technology Department, The WebQuest Page: http://webquest.sdsu.edu/matrix.html

Fisher, E. (1997). Educationally important types of children's talk. In R. Wegerif & P. Scrimshaw (Eds.), *Computers and talk in the primary classroom* (pp. 22-37). Clevedon, United Kingdom: Multilingual Matters, Ltd.

Gabbard, A. (n.d.). *A creative encounter of the numerical kind: A WebQuest for middle grade math students.* Retrieved February 20, 2002, from Northern Kentucky University, WebQuest Database: http://www.nku.edu/~webquest/gabbard/

Johnson, D. W., & Johnson, R. T. (n.d.). *Cooperative learning.* Retrieved February 1, 2002, from the University of Minnesota, The Cooperative Learning Center Web site: http://www.clcrc.com/pages/cl.html

Jonassen, D. H., Hernandez-Serrano, J., & Choi, I. (2000). Integrating constructivism and learning technologies. In J. M. Spector & T. M. Anderson (Eds.), *Integrated and holistic perspectives on learning, instruction and technology: Understanding complexity* (pp. 103-128). Dordrecht, The Netherlands: Kluwer.

Lee, M. (1993). Gender, group composition, and peer interaction in computer-based cooperative learning. *Journal of Educational Computing Research, 9,* 549-577.

National Council of Teachers of Mathematics. (1991). *Professional standards for teaching mathematics.* Reston, VA: Author.

National Council of Teachers of Mathematics. (2000). *Principles and standards for school mathematics.* Reston, VA: Author.

Ogle, D. M. (1986). K-W-L: A teaching model that develops active reading of expository text. *The Reading Teacher, 39,* 564-570.

Scrimshaw, P., & Perkins, G. (1997). Tinker Town: Working together. In R. Wegerif & P. Scrimshaw (Eds.), *Computers and talk in the primary classroom* (pp. 113-132). Clevedon, United Kingdom: Multilingual Matters, Ltd.

Swann, J. (1997). Tinker Town: Reading and re-reading children's talk around the computer. In R. Wegerif & P. Scrimshaw (Eds.), *Computers and talk in the primary classroom* (pp. 133-150). Clevedon, United Kingdom: Multilingual Matters, Ltd.

Tiessen, E. L., & Ward, D. R. (1997). Collaboration by design: Context, structure, and medium. *Journal of Interactive Learning Research, 8,* 175-197.

Watson, M. (1997a). Improving group work at computers. In R. Wegerif & P. Scrimshaw (Eds.), *Computers and talk in the primary classroom* (pp. 211-225). Clevedon, United Kingdom: Multilingual Matters, Ltd.

Watson, M. (1997b). The gender issue: Is what you see what you get? In R. Wegerif & P. Scrimshaw (Eds.), *Computers and talk in the primary classroom* (pp. 151-167). Clevedon, United Kingdom: Multilingual Matters, Ltd.

Wegerif, R., & Mercer, N. (1997). A dialogical framework for researching peer talk. In R. Wegerif & P. Scrimshaw (Eds.), *Computers and talk in the primary classroom* (pp. 49-61). Clevedon, United Kingdom: Multilingual Matters, Ltd.

Wegerif, R., & Scrimshaw, P. (1997). Introduction: Computers in the classroom context. In R. Wegerif & P. Scrimshaw (Eds.), *Computers and talk in the primary classroom* (pp. 1-9). Clevedon, United Kingdom: Multilingual Matters, Ltd.

Irene Chen
Jerry Willis
Sue Mahoney

WebCT and Its Growth
as a Type II Application

SUMMARY. Maddux, Johnson, and Willis mentioned in 1992 some "yet-to-be-developed types" that "have the potential to be Type II software if they are used in such a way that the user is given the ability to learn in new and better ways." The authors of this paper will frame the discussion of learning management systems (LMS) around the concept of Type I and Type II applications of computers in education. We suggest that with the new trends of interoperability within WebCT, more researchers will accept WebCT as a potential Type II application. As more interactive learning objects are developed and shared on the WebCT format, it should be easier for instructors to create and teach courses that reflect the value systems expressed in the concept of Type II learning. *[Article copies available for a fee from The Haworth Document Delivery Service: 1-800-HAWORTH. E-mail address: <docdelivery@haworthpress.com> Website: <http://www.HaworthPress.com> © 2005 by The Haworth Press, Inc. All rights reserved.]*

IRENE CHEN is Assistant Professor, Department of Urban Education, University of Houston Downtown, Houston, TX 77002 (E-mail: cheni@uhd.edu).
JERRY WILLIS is Professor, Department of Educational Leadership, Research, & Counseling, Louisiana State University, Baton Rouge, LA 70803 (E-mail: jerryw@lsu.edu).
SUE MAHONEY is Assistant Professor, Department of Urban Education, University of Houston Downtown, Houston, TX 77002 (E-mail: mahoneys@uhd.edu).

[Haworth co-indexing entry note]: "WebCT and Its Growth as a Type II Application." Chen, Irene, Jerry Willis, and Sue Mahoney. Co-published simultaneously in *Computers in the Schools* (The Haworth Press, Inc.) Vol. 22, No. 1/2, 2005, pp. 147-156; and: *Internet Applications of Type II Uses of Technology in Education* (ed: Cleborne D. Maddux, and D. LaMont Johnson) The Haworth Press, Inc., 2005, pp. 147-156. Single or multiple copies of this article are available for a fee from The Haworth Document Delivery Service [1-800-HAWORTH, 9:00 a.m. - 5:00 p.m. (EST). E-mail address: docdelivery@haworthpress.com].

Available online at http://www.haworthpress.com/web/CITS
© 2005 by The Haworth Press, Inc. All rights reserved.
Digital Object Identifier: 10.1300/J025v22n01_13

KEYWORDS. CMI (computer-managed instruction), IMS (instructional management systems), interactive games, LMS (learning management systems), Mindtools, multimedia authoring software, reusable learning objects, WebCT, Type I applications, Type II applications

As of January 2004, WebCT (Web Course Tools, http://www.webct.com) was available in 14 major world languages and thousands of institutions in over 85 countries were licensed to use it. There are, of course, other course management systems in widespread use in higher education, including Blackboard, but most of them share many common characteristics. We will use the details of WebCT to explore the implications of using learning management systems (LMS) in teacher education. LMS are already well established in higher education and seem poised to expand from higher education to K-12 education (Westhoff, 2003). We will look at the *way* LMS are and can be used and discuss the "worthiness" of the different types of use. This focus seems more appropriate since WebCT is not a single-purpose tool; it is capable of supporting many different types of courses and many forms of teacher/student and student/student interactions.

A BRIEF REVIEW OF CLASSIFICATIONS
OF EDUCATIONAL SOFTWARE BY FUNCTIONS

Since the 1980s, Maddux, Johnson, and Willis have attempted to categorize all educational computing as either Type I or Type II applications (Eastmond & Granger, 1998). *The Computing Teacher*, an educational computing journal (February 1987), even featured the Type I/Type II conceptual framework on its cover. In all three editions of *Educational Computing: Learning with Tomorrow's Technologies*, Maddux, Johnson, and Willis defined Type I applications as software that is designed to make it easier, quicker, or otherwise more efficient to continue teaching topics in the same ways they have always been taught (Maddux, Johnson, & Willis, 1992; Maddux, Johnson, & Willis, 1997; Maddux, Johnson, & Willis, 2001). Type I applications include the use of technology for drill and practice, tutorials, assessment, as well as administrative applications, and computer-managed instruction (CMI). In contrast, Type II applications make available new and better ways of teaching and are treated as more important and more significant ways to use technology in education (Maddux, Johnson, & Willis, 2001). Type

II applications include word processing, electronic spreadsheets, database management, programming language, simulations, problem solving, computers as prosthetic aides for the handicapped, and telecommunications.

In a similar way, Jonassen (1995; 2000) described *Mindtools* as knowledge representation tools that use computer applications to engage learners in critical thinking. *Mindtools* allow learners to enter into an intellectual partnership with the computer that allows them to begin to interpret information in new ways. He also categorized the use of computers in classrooms as "learning from computers: computer-assisted instruction, learning about computers: computer literacy, and learning with computers: a constructivist perspective" (p. xiii). *Learning from computers* is characterized as computer-assisted instruction and is composed of drill and practice, tutorials, and intelligent tutoring systems. This category parallels the Type I applications discussed by Maddux, Johnson, and Willis (1992; 1997; 2001). *Learning about computers*, computer literacy, does not have a counterpart in the Maddux, Johnson, and Willis classification system, but *learning with computers* closely resembles their Type II applications.

These two schools of thought share many similarities. The Type I/Type II system, as Maddux, Johnson, and Willis (2001) claimed, "embodies an educational value system judgment, whereas traditional categorizations are merely descriptive" (p. 99). The term *Mindtools* itself, in contrast to traditional applications, implies a value judgment as well because more important cognitive activities are supported and fostered. The key attributes of Mindtools are very similar to the attributes of Type II applications. Type II applications can function as intellectual partners with the learner in order to engage and facilitate critical thinking and higher order learning. Effective Type II applications are also generalizable computer tools that are intended to engage and facilitate cognitive processing. In a similar vein, Perkins' (1991) analysis of the way constructivism and technology may "make a marriage" divides computer applications into five different types: information banks, symbol pads, construction kits, phenomenonaria, and task managers. While the terminology is different these can be Type II applications. We say "can be" because virtually all the examples given for Mindtools, constructivist uses of technology, and Type II applications can be used in ways that are much more traditional and standard, in other words, Type I uses. We will suggest in this paper that, while some characteristics of WebCT and other LMS support Type II uses, the factor that determines whether a particular instance of WebCT use is Type I or Type II has less to do with whether LMS are used and more with the *way* they are used.

WEBCT AND TYPE II APPLICATIONS

We have taken the position that it is the way programs like WebCT *are used* that determines whether the use is Type I or Type II. However, it is true that some types of educational software were clearly developed for and are most suited to Type I or Type II uses. The early versions of WebCT and competing programs like Blackboard also seem most suited to Type I applications. However, when considering the types of uses WebCT can support, it may be helpful to at least envision what WebCT will be like in the next five to ten years.

New kinds of tools are currently being developed to use with WebCT. These new technologies allow for the extension and enhancement of course design and delivery capabilities of WebCT (Bray & Boufford, 2003). For example, in August 2004, WebCT and MERLOT announced a strategic partnership to facilitate *inter-institution learning content exchange.* MERLOT (Multimedia Educational Resource for Learning and Online Teaching, http://www.merlot.org) is one of the major clearinghouses of higher-education online content that make materials available online (http://www.merlot.org) to anyone without charge. To better understand the capabilities of several of these innovative tools, a brief explanation/discussion has been included to cover e-packs, reusable learning objects, interactive games, multimedia authoring tools, and WebCT PowerLinks. These new technologies are incorporated to expand student control over the WebCT learning environment (Bray & Boufford, 2003).

E-pack. Currently, one of the widest-known third-party tools that can be embedded within a LMS is the e-pack. WebCT offers over 2,000 e-packs in more than 50 subject areas with support from major textbook publishers (WebCT, 2004). These course packs offer a course structure and set of readings developed by publishers, along with a distribution agreement with WebCT. E-packs can contain a variety of features including a question database, interactive media, critical-thinking activities, instructor resources, flashcards, glossary, videos, animations, and an e-book. To facilitate the sharing of content within and among institutions, WebCT has developed a content migration utility that allows content and assessment information to be imported or exported from WebCT courses (WebCT, 2004).

Reusable learning objects. A reusable learning object (RLO) is modular, free-standing, able to satisfy a single learning objective, and transportable among applications and environments. As organizations make significant investments in digital learning content, they seek greater assurances of portability, platform independence, longevity, and reusability of digital content (Resnick, 2002). The development and acceptance of open standards help safeguard investments in content development because they enable integration with other campus systems and facilitate content sharing.

Interactive games. The integration of interactive games with LMS is another interesting technology trend. !MPACT 2003, the fifth Annual WebCT Users' Conference held in San Diego, served as the catalyst for the creation of the Digital Games Community (http://www.webct.com/games) which is hosted on WebCT space (Bray & Boufford, 2003). WebCT has foreseen the growing emphasis on interactivity in online educational games. The use of digital games has attracted the interest of many educators who are interested in using games to enhance learning through shared ideas, experiences, resources, and best practices (Bray & Boufford, 2003).

Multimedia authoring software. WebCT is also working with multimedia authoring software companies to make the software output compatible with the XML formats and the instructional management systems (IMS) e-learning specifications. Instruction designers or teachers will need to have multimedia authoring software such as Hot Potatoes™ and Lectora® to create interactive games that will work with WebCT. The Hot Potatoes™ Suite (2004) is a project of the Half-Baked Software group (http://web.uvic.ca/hrd/halfbaked/) and is available without charge for nonprofit use. It includes six applications, enabling users to create interactive multiple-choice, short-answer, jumbled-sentence, crossword, matching/ordering, and gap-fill exercises for the Web. A more versatile product is the commercial package, Lectora Publisher,® which is a multimedia authoring tool (http://www.lectora.com/product_info_overview.html). It is used to create interactive learning objects such as puzzles, drag-and-drop types of quiz questions, and the connection type of questions. Unfortunately, both Hot Potatoes™ and Lectora® are clearly designed to make it easier to create and use Web-based learning activities that are predominately Type I. Using either of these products with WebCT enhances the power of WebCT as a Type I tool, but does not significantly expand Type II potential.

However, while neither Hot Potatoes™ nor Lectora® Publisher are highly supportive of Type II uses, we believe they are the vanguard of more sophisticated and more flexible authoring systems that will be available in the near future. One reason the current generation of authoring packages supports Type I uses so well is that it is far easier to create such packages. The same was true of drill-and-practice and tutorial software in the late 1970s and 1980s when educational computing became popular. Hundreds of thousands of math drill programs were written and distributed, for example, but today there are many excellent Type II applications of computer technology in mathematics, including simulations and problem-based activities. We expect that same type of development to occur in the tools that help you create content for programs like WebCT.

WebCT PowerLinks. Another set of tools to enhance the interoperability is PowerLinks, which makes it possible for external applications to interface with WebCT e-learning platforms. Course designers can choose from partner-developed PowerLinks or even incorporate their own custom applications. PowerLinks is flexible in that it allows you to link WebCT courses to many different types of programs.

The additional flexibility afforded by the ability to use e-packs, integrate reusable learning objects, build interactive games, create content with multimedia authoring tools, and use PowerLinks all add to the potential of programs like WebCT. Many of these new tools are simply more efficient or more interesting ways to offer Type I instruction. Some, however, allow more student control and more creative interaction with the content as well as more student-to-student interaction. We believe the second and third generations of these tools will be even more Type II friendly.

AN EXAMPLE:
THE USE OF WEBCT
IN A TEACHER EDUCATION PROGRAM

A look at how WebCT is used in a teacher education program will help to explain the current state of WebCT and the implications of the new trends that will be brought about by WebCT in the near future. MAT 6318, Advanced Educational Technology, is a course in the Master of Arts in Teaching program in a southwestern university. Most of the students in this course are teachers in urban schools with varying degrees of technology competence. MAT 6318 focuses on technology from each of three perspectives: as a *tool*, as a *medium*, and as a *setting* for learning. WebCT is used in MAT 6318 as a Web-based LMS that helps support the classroom learning community. The flexibility of WebCT gives more control to students both in terms of *how* (sequence, pace, next steps) they study as well as *what* they study. Thus, WebCT helps support an approach to the course that has a number of Type II characteristics, even though the basic WebCT system was created with Type I uses in mind.

For typical Type II applications, many hours are generally necessary for a user to discover everything a specific program is capable of doing. This is true for first-time WebCT users. As the WebCT interface becomes more transparent to them, they focus on the course activities and their interaction with the content, the instructors, and other students. Many students are comfortable treating the course, and the support provided by WebCT components, as Type I activities that require them to "do what the teacher says and take the test." It requires some effort and encouragement to move these students from that mode of thinking to a more Type II mode in which they take more responsibility for what they learn. However, the same can probably be said of instructors who use WebCT. It is much easier to create a WebCT course that reflects Type I values and approaches than a Type II course. Encouragement along with the availability of tools that support Type II uses as well as examples of Type II courses in resource libraries like MERLOT should encourage more instructors to explore ways of moving from Type I to Type II learning environments, even for their distance education courses. Furthermore, with the new trend of interoperability, more interactive learning objects will be written for the WebCT environment. These new additions will require that users spend more time exploring the many features built into the activities. In summary, more interactive learning objects can be added to WebCT to extend its capability to interact with learners and "make new and better ways of teaching and learning available to teachers and students," which are characteristics of Type II applications (Maddux, Johnson, & Willis, 1992, p. 26).

DISCUSSION

WebCT was not mentioned in the 1992 version of *Educational Computing: Learning with Tomorrow's Technologies* because the company was not in existence at that time, but it was discussed in the assessment category of Type I applications in the 2001, third edition of the book. Maddux, Johnson, and Willis (2001) simply stated that some characteristics of Type I or Type II applications are difficult to apply to this class of software.

If WebCT is scrutinized with the 1992 definition, it matches most of the characteristics of CMI, and therefore falls in the category of Type I. Maddux, Johnson, and Willis (1992, 2001) described CMI as "a mixed bag of applications designed to perform tasks or combinations of tasks such as organizing student data, monitoring student progress, testing student mastery and prescribing further instruction or remediation, recording student progress, and selecting the order of instructional modules to be completed" (1992, p. 30; 2001, p. 108). However, in the meantime, WebCT is also a type of telecommunications application, which is an example of Type II applications according to the definitions of both 1992 and 2001.

It is interesting to observe the classification of telecommunications software as it may shed some light on calling WebCT a Type II application. Maddux, Johnson, and Willis (1992) listed the following software as Type II applications: word processing, electronic spreadsheets, database management, programming languages, simulations, problem-solving software, and computers as prosthetic aids for the handicapped. They wrote: "Type II applications, like Type I applications, vary considerably" (p. 26). At the end of the discussion, graphics software, presentation software, and telecommunications were briefly mentioned as "having potential" to be Type II applications: "Telecommunications software enables more than one computer to be linked. These types of software, as well as other yet to be developed types, have the potential to be Type II software if they are used in such a way that the user is given the ability to learn in new and better ways" (p. 39). Having witnessed the growth of the Internet, Maddux, Johnson, and Willis in their 2001 edition added a new section that explained telecommunications software as a Type II application.

The authors believe that with the new trends of interoperability within WebCT, more and more researchers will accept WebCT as a potential Type II application. The fulfillment of that potential is, however, dependent on two things. First, instructors must be willing to design and implement courses that reflect the use of Type II concepts. WebCT, and other LMS, can easily be used to create drills, tutorials, and other forms of instruction that simply put online the traditional methods of teaching (lecture, demonstration) of traditional content. It is still (and may always be) more difficult to design and implement Type II coursework. The *way* resources and tools, including WebCT, are used determines whether learning is Type I or Type II. For example, using word processing as a secretarial substitute for keyboarding is a Type I application. However, using word processing to teach creative writing skills is a Type II application (Maddux, Johnson, & Willis, 2001). As more interactive learning objects are developed and shared on the WebCT format, and as more tools are developed to facilitate the creation of Type II activities, it should be easier for instructors to create and teach courses that reflect the value system expressed in the concept of Type II learning.

Maddux, Johnson, and Willis (1992) mentioned some "yet to be developed types" that "have the potential to be Type II software if they are used in such a way that the user is given the ability to learn in new and better ways" (p. 39). The 1992, 1997, and 2001 editions of the Type I/Type II categorization systems reflect the state of the art during the time when the books were published. The concept will continue to change as rapidly as the technologies that underlie it. With the new trends that expand student control over the learning environment, WebCT can now be used as a Type II application, in the same manner as telecommunications has developed new flexibility and power, and thus has been re-categorized as a Type II application.

As WebCT undergoes changes, the current authors believe that it would be extremely difficult to teach the same course of MAT 6318 without using WebCT, because WebCT has been used in such a way that it makes new and better ways of teaching possible, which reinforces WebCT as a Type II application. Whether WebCT becomes a powerful and preferred Type II application is another matter. Australian educator Martin Dougiamas decided the limitations of WebCT and similar programs were so serious that he developed Moodle (http://moodle.org/) a free, open-source online course management system designed specifically for constructivist, and thus Type II, learning. While Moodle is not as polished as WebCT and other commercial LMS, it relies on freely available software and is available in 40 languages. We do not know whether Microsoft's Windows or Linux operating systems will dominate the future of computing, and we do not know whether programs like Moodle will overwhelm WebCT, but we can be sure that the development environments for both will continue to evolve in directions that make creating and using Type II applications easier and more interesting.

REFERENCES

Bray, B., & Boufford, B. (2003). *Having fun learning WebCT using games to enhance training*. Retrieved February 27, 2004, from http://booboo.webct.com/2003/papers/Bray.pdf

Eastmond, D., & Granger, D. (1998, March 8). Using Type II computer network technology to reach distance students. *Distance Education Report*, 2(3), 1-3.

The Hot Potatoes™ Suite. (2004). http://web.uvic.ca/hrd/halfbaked/

Jonassen, D. H. (1995). *Computers in the classroom: Mindtools for critical thinking.* Upper Saddle River, NJ: Prentice Hall.

Jonassen, D. (2000). *Computers as mindtools for schools: Engaging critical thinking* (2nd ed.). Upper Saddle River: NJ: Merrill-Prentice Hall.

Maddux, C., Johnson, D. L., & Willis, J. (1992). *Educational computing: Learning with tomorrow's technologies.* Needham Heights, MA: Allyn & Bacon.

Maddux, C., Johnson, D. L., & Willis, J. (1997). *Educational computing: Learning with tomorrow's technologies* (2nd ed.). Needham Heights, MA: Allyn & Bacon.

Maddux, C., Johnson, D. L., & Willis, J. (2001). *Educational computing: Learning with tomorrow's technologies* (3rd ed.). Needham Heights, MA: Allyn & Bacon.

MERLOT, Multimedia Educational Resource for Learning and Online Teaching. (2004). http://www.merlot.org/Home.po

Perkins, D. N. (1991). Technology meets constructivism: Do they make a marriage. *Educational Technology, 13,* 18-23.

Resnick, M. (2002). Rethinking learning in the digital age. In G. Kirkman, J. D. Sachs, K. Schwab, & P. K. Cornelius (Eds.), *Global information technology report: Readiness for the networked world.* Oxford: Oxford University Press.

Westhoff, G. (2003). Training preservice students to utilize Web-based portfolios and select appropriate bodies of evidence. *Society for Information Technology and Teacher Education International Conference 2003*(1), 206-209.

WebCT. (2004, August 4). WebCT and MERLOT form strategic partnership to energize inter-institution learning content exchange. Retrieved September 14, 2004, from http://www.webct.com/service/ViewContent?contentID=22334284

WebCT. (2004). Retrieved January 27, 2004, from http://www.webct.com

Elizabeth Chaney
David Alan Gilman

Filling in the Blanks:
Using Computers to Test and Teach

SUMMARY. This paper reviews the history of technology and testing. The role and functions of computers in education have become more varied, from drill and practice to simple tutorials to WebQuests. However, one important aspect of teaching for which the computer is ideally suited, achievement testing, is often overlooked. While it is not difficult to envision computers administering and scoring tests, there is also learning that occurs when tests are administered by a computer. Advantages and disadvantages of computer-based testing are also examined. Finally Type II applications are explored. *[Article copies available for a fee from The Haworth Document Delivery Service: 1-800-HAWORTH. E-mail address: <docdelivery@ haworthpress.com> Website: <http://www.HaworthPress.com> © 2005 by The Haworth Press, Inc. All rights reserved.]*

KEYWORDS. Computers in education, advantages/disadvantages of computer-based testing, Type II applications, history of technology and testing

---

ELIZABETH CHANEY is Assistant Professor, Department of Curriculum, Instruction, and Media Technology, School of Education, Indiana State University, Terre Haute, IN 47809 (E-mail: eschaney@isugw.indstate.edu).
DAVID ALAN GILMAN is Professor, College of Education, Oakland City University, Oakland City, IN 47620 (E-mail: efgilman@hotmail.com).

[Haworth co-indexing entry note]: "Filling in the Blanks: Using Computers to Test and Teach." Chaney, Elizabeth, and David Alan Gilman. Co-published simultaneously in *Computers in the Schools* (The Haworth Press, Inc.) Vol. 22, No. 1/2, 2005, pp. 157-168; and: *Internet Applications of Type II Uses of Technology in Education* (ed: Cleborne D. Maddux, and D. LaMont Johnson) The Haworth Press, Inc., 2005, pp. 157-168. Single or multiple copies of this article are available for a fee from The Haworth Document Delivery Service [1-800-HAWORTH, 9:00 a.m. - 5:00 p.m. (EST). E-mail address: docdelivery@haworthpress.com].

Available online at http://www.haworthpress.com/web/CITS
© 2005 by The Haworth Press, Inc. All rights reserved.
Digital Object Identifier: 10.1300/J025v22n01_14

The role and functions of computers in education have become more varied, from drill and practice to simple tutorials to WebQuests. However, one important aspect of teaching for which the computer is ideally suited, achievement testing, is often overlooked. While it is not difficult to envision computers administering and scoring tests, there is also learning that occurs when tests are administered via a computer (Van Horn, 2003).

A small percentage of educators have proposed abolishing tests, and some teachers consider tests to be nothing more than a necessary evil (Ebel, 1965). However, most teachers believe that tests are a vital component in the instructional process. It is not difficult for most educators, after contemplation, to agree with a statement attributed to the late Robert Ebel. Ebel asserted, "It is probably not extravagant to say that the contribution made to a student's store of knowledge by the taking of an examination is as great, minute for minute, as any other enterprise he engages in" (Ebel, 1965; Ebel, 1972).

Testing has many components that are valuable in the instructional process: diagnosis, evaluation, prognosis, reinforcement, and knowledge of results. Learning through testing occurs as students receive immediate feedback that is appropriate to the responses they have made and as they are reinforced for correct responses (Skinner, 1954).

Regardless of how one feels about the importance of testing, it should be obvious that facilitating the learning process should involve the assessment of student learning (Roos, 1997). It should also be obvious that computers can play an important role in that process (Derousa & Fleming, 1999).

HISTORY OF TECHNOLOGY AND TESTING

The foundations of technology, testing, and teaching are deeply interwoven. In the early 1920s, Sidney Pressey (1926) invented a device that tested students and provided instruction through what Pressey called "adjunct auto-instruction." The device presented questions, evaluated the correctness of the response, gave students immediate and appropriate feedback, and proceeded to the next question. Although Sidney Pressey is given credit for having invented the "teaching machine," he originally described his invention as "a machine that gives tests–and teaches" (Pressey, 1926, p. 35). To simplify adjunct auto-instruction, Pressey also presented tests in a format described as the "Pressey Punchboard." To Pressey, the important function of the machine was that it gave tests; teaching was just a bonus. However, because of the Great Depression and the accompanying surplus of teachers, Pressey's teaching machine did not get off to a good start and was not well received by the education profession (Pressey, 1963). Nevertheless, countless research studies have demonstrated the value of adjunct auto-instruction and the instructional strategy of testing by machine (Derousa & Fleming, 1998; Bocij & Greasley, 1999; Van Horn, 2003).

Before the advent of microcomputers, there were several devices marketed that followed the strategy of Pressey's original machine. Two of these were the Didactor and Teach 'N Test, marketed by the Didactics Corporation of Mansfield, Ohio, and used for providing training in a variety of industries. These quasi-computers were sequenced by programs that were controlled by rays of light shining through transparent spaces in dark film. Although this device seems primitive when compared to computers today, the actual operation of the machine was not unlike that of the punch cards used in computers of the next generation.

Another device, popular with elementary students, was the Tutorgram, marketed by the Enrichment Reaching Corporation of America (ERCA) of Iron Ridge, Wisconsin. The Tutorgram used cards with holes in them placed on a live electronic grid. Although feedback for correct and incorrect answers was provided with a flashing light or a buzzer, the Tutorgram did not actually keep score. It only provided activities that were primarily drill and practice.

It is surprising that even in today's economy, the adaptation of Pressey's invention to computers has been so slow in coming because testing via computer has various desirable features that paper-and-pencil testing does not possess. These features assist the instructor to reduce many frustrations with testing and to release the instructor from mundane and laborious tasks such as repetitive grading and the creation of tests with random questions (Derousa & Fleming, 1999; Vispoel, 2000; Van Horn, 2003).

Several commercially marketed test-generating programs, such as Test-Maker, eTest, MicroCAT, and Test Suite are available. Course management programs such as Blackboard, also known as CourseInfo, and WebCT contain subprograms that manage, administer, and score tests. These programs make it possible for instructors to choose from multiple choice, true/false, matching, sentence completion, short answer, and even essay items.

Advantages of Computerized Testing

Grade book. There are many advantages to testing students by use of computers. Most computer-testing software packages include a grade book feature to help the instructor keep track of student progress. When students take tests by computer, their test scores can be automatically recorded in the teacher's grade book. With a grade book, teachers can record scores, compute weighted averages, and create graphs and charts to depict how students performed. It is no longer necessary for teachers to use a calculator or to manually perform arithmetic when they are computing test scores and averages. Teachers are now released from hours of grading. This feature greatly reduces the amount of time teachers spend in the testing process and frees teachers so that they can devote more time to creative tasks such as lesson planning, professional study, and developing creative classroom activities.

Statistical analysis. For those teachers who tremble at the mention of the word *statistics*, the grade books, which are a part of computerized testing, allow teachers to statistically analyze their tests and student progress. Statistical analyses can be performed on the scores of individual students or classes as a whole and individual items or entire tests. Item analyses can be performed to determine the characteristics of individual test items, and the quality of a test can be determined by test analysis.

The analysis of individual student performance provides instructors with scores, averages, weighted averages, and mastery determination. Grades can be assigned according to a predetermined formula. Item analysis provides instructors with indices of the relative difficulty and discrimination power of individual test items so that the test can be improved the next time it is to be administered. Test analysis provides information concerning the quality of the test, such as various reliability coefficients and the standard error of measurement. All of this statistical data are being calculated even as the computer is administering and scoring the test.

Asynchronous practice tests. Another use of computer testing is in performing drill-and-practice exercises in which computer-based testing is used in a purely didactic way. This activity is not particularly useful for measuring student achievement, but it serves as valuable supplemental instruction or as a review for major examinations. With computer-based testing, students may take practice tests asynchronously. In other words, they may complete the practice tests at any time. Students may also repeat the practice test as many times as they wish in an attempt to enhance their learning and to increase their performance on scheduled examinations.

Instructors can set up tests that require students to begin and end the test at certain times. No longer do instructors have to worry about students continuing to work past the bell. Students are able to monitor their progress and also time themselves.

One strategy used in computer-based testing is the self-scoring test. In this instructional strategy, the student is required to respond to each question until that question is answered correctly. The machine will guide the learner to the next question after–but only after–the preceding question is answered correctly. Scoring is similar to the scoring system in golf. Each student's score is the number of responses that student required to answer all of the test items correctly (Gilman & Ferry, 1972).

Laws of learning. Computer-based testing takes advantage of some of the contingencies that are expressed in so-called laws of learning. In this context, the laws are paraphrased in terms that are related to the process of computer-based testing. The first of these is the Law of Effect: Responses to questions that are followed by reinforcement are remembered and learned. The second is the Law of Exercise, which states that the more often responses to test questions are repeated, the more likely they are to be repeated. The third is the Law of Recency, which states that learners tend to repeat their most recent response to a question the next time the question appears (Skinner, 1954).

Randomization of items. Testing via computers allows instructors to give students test questions in a certain order and to randomize the questions. When the sequence of test items is randomly generated, each student is presented the test items in a different sequence. This makes it much more difficult for students to collaborate on the test since they cannot refer to items on the test by their numbers.

Remote control of computer testing. Through the Internet, tests can be created at any time, and the dates they will be given can be scheduled at any time. The tests may be created and edited at a remote location, as well.

Test administration. Teachers can administer tests via the Internet to students in various locations, but tests can also be administered to classes of students who are convened in a computer laboratory. With the use of computer software, education facilitators can choose when to release an exam and to whom the exam is released. Many teachers may choose to have the exam installed only on certain computers; whereas others may have the exam available via a network requiring a username and password to access the test.

Exams can be offered over a period of three to five days so that students can schedule them at a convenient time. This not only frees up class time for instruction but also eliminates the necessity to schedule make-up exams. Students who have experienced long periods of absence can readily be accommodated by scheduling testing times.

Scoring. Today, teachers no longer find it necessary to lug home stacks of multiple choice exams to grade over the weekend. Blackboard and WebCT allow the instructor to choose whether he/she prefers for the exam to be scored immediately after the student takes the test or to wait until the instructor gives the command to the computer to score it. Tests can also be scored by hand. With just the click of a mouse, an entire class's tests can be graded and the results entered into the instructor's spreadsheet grade book. Examinations graded by computer reduce the chance for error, and teachers are given more time to focus on areas such as lesson planning and individualized instruction.

Immediate feedback. Throughout the history of teaching by machine there has been controversy concerning one of the obvious advantages: immediate feedback, or what is sometimes called the knowledge of results. Although B. F. Skinner (1954) predicted that there would be a significant reduction in learning if feedback was delayed for as little as six seconds, other psychologists challenged his reasoning. They pointed to the beneficial effects of feedback, even when it is delayed for several hours. Nevertheless, if instructors wish to have student learning increase by providing immediate knowledge of whether their responses were correct, computer testing is necessary (Roos, 1997).

Computerized testing provides immediate feedback through its self-scoring capability. Students can receive feedback immediately and know the results of their testing. While educational psychologists disagree on the importance of immediate feedback in the learning process, students and teachers readily agree that it is a convenience they prefer (Vispoel, 2000).

Role in distance education. Through the invention of computerized testing, distance education has taken a step away from the correspondence schools of the past. Students can now be hundreds of miles away from their instructors while they are tested over material that has been covered in their distance education classes. As the proximity of teacher to student decreases, issues of testing security increase. Nevertheless, remote testing clearly offers options to students who are unable to travel to the testing location for one reason or another.

Use of multimedia in testing. Graphics, either in still or motion form, can be used in the computer-based testing procedure. Bennett, Goodman, Hessinger, Kahn, Ligget, Marshall, and Zack (1999) described many ways to use multimedia in testing situations.

Dissemination of testing. The test can be distributed to numerous students at one time via the Internet. The instructor is able to select when and to which students the test will be released. Instructors can simultaneously administer tests to students who are on campus and those who are in remote locations. Although the best practices from a testing standpoint occur when all students are administered the same test, at the same location, and at the same time, it is also possible for students to complete tests according to their own time schedule through a process that is called *asynchronous learning*. With computer testing, it is also possible for instructors to place a time schedule and a time limit on the examination.

Recording of grades. With the use of computers to test students, instructors can set up courses to grade tests for students and to keep track of their test scores. Students no longer need to continually approach teachers with the questions, "How did I do on the last test?" and "What grade am I getting in your class?" With computers, a student can simply look on the course Web site to find the answers to those questions.

Efficiency. Computerized testing saves time because instructors can reuse good questions from old tests. Changes can be made quickly, and the time instructors would have devoted to writing new questions can be spent on more effective teaching and learning activities.

Quality. By carefully conducting item analyses and test analyses, instructors can weed out items that are too difficult and those that do not adequately discriminate between good and poor students. A good pool of items can be accumulated, and these can be drawn from for future tests.

Disadvantages of Computer-Based Testing

Heightened anxiety and student resistance. Although it is becoming less of a problem with each passing year, some students claim that they do not perform as well on computer examinations and claim that being tested at a computer heightens their anxiety (Powers, 2001). However, Johnson, Enerson, and Plank (1998) cite studies performed at Pennsylvania State University in which students were permitted to take the same test on paper after they took it on the computer. These experiments have shown conclusively that student scores have little to do with the form of testing.

Cheating. Instructors who use computers to test their students often worry about their students cheating. Instructors ask themselves questions such as, "How do I know my students are the ones taking my exams?" or "How do I know that my student is not using information from the Internet or other sources to help him do well on my test?" At first, computer-based testing may seem to require the instructor to relinquish some control of the testing process.

However, there are mechanisms educators may employ to secure testing trustworthiness. Students can be given individual usernames and passwords before each test to access it via the computer. Tests can be timed to allow a student only enough time to answer the question without extra minutes to find additional information on the Web. Short answer and essay questions can be worded to require the student to personalize the answer to reduce plagiarism. The test can be offered only on certain computers at certain locations or in reserved labs at particular times.

The following paragraph, taken from Johnson, Enerson, and Plank (1998), describes the lengths instructors go to in order to ensure that testing is administered fairly:

> Photo IDs are checked at the door and names matched to those on the class roster. Students sit in booths around the perimeter of the room with the proctor at the center of the room. Each student is presented the same questions but in random order. Students are not allowed to bring paper into the facility or take paper out, but they are given scratch paper to write on during the exam. Participants asked what would prevent students from smuggling out questions and answers. Presenters responded that while students may manage to copy or memorize a few questions and the answer choices, most find this difficult and not worth the effort. Because the questions are presented in random order, some students are initially convinced that their peers took a different exam. Test scores have been highly consistent over the years suggesting that leakage does not occur. Because no paper copies of the exam exist, computerized testing practically eliminates fraternity test files. (p. 42)

Labor-intensive. While transferring a course from a traditional mode to an online one, instructors often feel overwhelmed. To begin with, the organization of the Web site must be considered. In addition, all lecture notes, exams, handouts, and supplementary materials have to be uploaded or typed onto the course Web site. For educators who have taught for years, many procedures, lectures, and commentaries have been transmitted orally to students in the classroom. As a course is being transformed to an online version, teachers find it difficult or time consuming to clearly communicate their intentions. The work for course transformations are clearly front-loaded. While one may feel frustrations setting up courses on the Web at the beginning of the semester, the freedom that is associated with computerized testing allows the instructor to be released from the drudgery of frantically grading papers and calculating scores at the end of the semester.

Transmission difficulties. While incorporating technology into the classroom can be efficient, it can also be extremely frustrating when it does not work correctly. Occasionally a glitch will occur and a student will not have access to the test. Or, if a student is absent and misses the timed test that was given on the computer, how does he/she retake it? If a teacher's computer fails to work properly, how does he/she administer the test to all students? These are logistical considerations to keep in mind when planning to test via computer. Inevitably, technology will not live up to expectations. How then will the instructor deal with the shortcomings? Always anticipate problems.

Software changes. Another disadvantage to computerized testing is that course software often does not interface. Once a course has been created in one program, it may not easily transfer to another program. When schools or universities purchase a licensing agreement, educators then upload their course information to particular software and eventually get comfortable using it. If the school changes programs, educators are often left with the nuisance of moving all of the course materials to the new software program. Sometimes this is easier said than done. Educators should encourage administrators to purchase software that allows easy transmission of materials from one learning system to another.

The Future of Computerized Testing

Resolving problems. There are still various problems that need to be resolved in order for the future of computerized testing to look brighter. Teachers still seem to have fears of losing their jobs to computerized testing. These fears need to be alleviated by showing them how instrumental teachers are to the success of computerized testing. Education has a history of resisting serious change, with some exceptions. This tendency to resist change lessens the motivation for software companies to develop the necessary programming needed for computerized testing. Software companies are beginning to demonstrate to educators how testing software does not eliminate the need for teachers; testing software greatly enhances teachers' abilities.

The advancement of computerized testing has been somewhat sluggish due to schools with large minority or low-income populations that are far less likely to have computers. Poor and minority children are much less likely to have computers at home, thus making it difficult to test via computer. However, reductions in the cost of computers are making large-scale computer delivery of tests increasingly more feasible for lower income schools.

When comparing computerized tests to paper-and-pencil tests, test-takers feel more constrained with computerized versions. Test-takers are unable to underline text, scratch out eliminated choices, and work out math problems–all commonly used strategies of test-takers. Software companies need to devise pop-up windows to allow students to "think" on the screen instead of on paper. As students are increasingly taking more tests via computer, they are feeling more at ease with the process.

Type II change. When computers were first used in the classroom, there was an "automation" approach to educational computing where computers were used to imitate the same behaviors and procedures that teachers do without the technology (Maddux, Johnson, & Willis, 2001). For instance, technology was used to create worksheets, to keep track of grades, to create PowerPoint presentations instead of using the blackboard or overheads, to post coursework and content online, to practice skills or learn new information through educational software, or to have online discussions. This, often called "Type I computer applications," makes traditional teaching methods easier, quicker, and more efficient.

For educators who desire to move a step beyond automation to creation and innovation, there are "Type II applications" that allow educators to teach in new and better ways–ways that are not possible without technology (Maddux, Johnson, & Willis, 2001). Type II uses of educational technology involve empowering students to do work they could not have done without technology. Instructors must look beyond how they can use technology for their teaching, to how students can use technology for their learning. Some examples of Type II applications are students using e-mail to contact authors or experts, using word-processing programs to learn to revise rough drafts, and creating media projects to facilitate sharing of information. Challenging oneself as an educator to move from Type I applications of technology to Type II applications can definitely reap many benefits for both teachers and students.

Summary. Sidney Pressey's invention is alive and well today but in a more sophisticated and technologically superior form. Many instructors are now experimenting with computer-based testing and are becoming aware of its convenience and advantages. As further developments in computer-based testing become available, the popularity of this genre of testing is bound to increase.

However, it is easy for those who recognize the logistical advantages of testing by computer to overlook its less obvious and more important function. The computer gives tests, but at the same time, it also teaches.

REFERENCES

Bennett, R., Goodman, M., Hessinger, J., Kahn, H., Ligget, J., Marshall, G., & Zack, J. (1999, May-July). Using multimedia in large-scale computer-based testing programs. *Computers in Human Behavior, 15*(3-4), 283-294.

Bocij, P., & Greasley, A. (1999, July). Can computer-based testing achieve quality and efficiency in assessment? *International Journal of Educational Computing, 1*(1), 1-15.

de Jager, P. (2004). Managing type II change. *The Galt Global Review.* Retrieved June 13, 2004, from http://www.galtglobalreview.com/careers/type_2_change.html

Derousa, E., & Fleming, M. (1998, November). A comparison of in-class quizzes vs. online. *Computers & Education, 31*(3), 281-300.

Ebel, R. L. (1965). *Measuring educational achievement.* Englewood Cliffs, NJ: Prentice Hall.

Ebel, R. L. (1972). *Essentials of measuring educational achievement.* Englewood Cliffs, NJ: Prentice Hall.

Gilman, D., & Ferry, P. (1972, Fall). Increasing test reliability through self-scoring procedures. *Journal of Educational Measurement, 9*(3), 503-507.

Johnson, R., Enerson, D., & Plank, K. (1998). Computerized testing roundtable. *Center for Excellence in Teaching & Learning.* Retrieved November 15, 2003, from http://www.psu.edu/celt/largeclass/comptest.html.

Maddux, C., Johnson, D., & Willis, J. (2001). *Educational computing: Learning with tomorrow's technologies.* Needham Heights, MA: Allyn & Bacon.

Powers, D. E. (2001) Test anxiety and test performance: Comparing paper-based and computer-adaptive versions of the Graduate Record Examination's (GRE) general test. (ERIC, Current Index to Journals in Education (CIJE) EJ63133)

Pressey, S. L. (1926). A simple device which gives tests and scores and teaches. *School and Society, 23*, 373-376.

Pressey, S. L. (1962). Basic unresolved teaching machine problems. *Theory into Practice, 1*, 30-37.

Roos, L. (1997, February). The role of item feedback in self-adapted testing. *Educational and Psychological Measurement, 57*(1), 85-98.

Skinner, B. F. (1954). The science of learning and the art of teaching. *Harvard Educational Review, 24*, 86-87.

Van Horn, R. (2003, April). Computer-adaptive tests and computer-based tests. *Phi Delta Kappan, 84*(8), 567, 630.

Vispoel, W. P. (2000, October). Computerized versus paper-and-pencil assignment of self concept: Score comparability and respondent preferences. *Measurement and Evaluation in Counseling and Development, 33*(3), 130-43.

Ian W. Gibson

Constructing Meaning in a Technology-Rich, Global Learning Environment

SUMMARY. This paper introduces the Global Forum on School Leadership (GFSL) as a Type II application of interactive computing technology suitable for 21st century learners, teachers, and school leaders. Simply put, the concept of the GFSL brings together learners who share a common goal, a common subject area, or a common profession, and encourages them to interact and learn together. Among the many differences that learners bring to the learning task, the one central and very obvious difference upon which the GFSL depends is culture. In the example presented here, the GFSL creates a learning partnership between a class of neophyte school leaders enrolled in a school leader preparation program in the United States and a similar class of students enrolled in a school leader preparation program in Australia (it could be anywhere else in the world). The discussion begins with a focus on the evolution of technology use in schools and the related evolution of learning in technologically rich environments. The GFSL is introduced as a Type II application increasingly necessary in a learning world where a

IAN W. GIBSON is Associate Professor and Unit Coordinator, Educational Leadership, Wichita State University, College of Education, Wichita, KS 67206-0142 (E-mail: ian.gibson@wichita.edu).

[Haworth co-indexing entry note]: "Constructing Meaning in a Technology-Rich, Global Learning Environment." Gibson, Ian W. Co-published simultaneously in *Computers in the Schools* (The Haworth Press, Inc.) Vol. 22, No. 1/2, 2005, pp. 169-182; and: *Internet Applications of Type II Uses of Technology in Education* (ed: Cleborne D. Maddux, and D. LaMont Johnson) The Haworth Press, Inc., 2005, pp. 169-182. Single or multiple copies of this article are available for a fee from The Haworth Document Delivery Service [1-800-HAWORTH, 9:00 a.m. - 5:00 p.m. (EST). E-mail address: docdelivery@haworthpress.com].

Available online at http://www.haworthpress.com/web/CITS
© 2005 by The Haworth Press, Inc. All rights reserved.
Digital Object Identifier: 10.1300/J025v22n01_15   169

global focus is being forced upon learners and where global understanding and awareness is becoming a basic survival skill. The paper generates a global version of the five characteristics of Type II applications, and concludes with an analysis of the impact of the Global Forum on participants' learning experiences and professional skills. *[Article copies available for a fee from The Haworth Document Delivery Service: 1-800-HAWORTH. E-mail address: <docdelivery@haworthpress.com> Website: <http://www.HaworthPress.com> © 2005 by The Haworth Press, Inc. All rights reserved.]*

KEYWORDS. Global, learning, interactive, technology, Type II applications, leadership, preparation programs, culture, pedagogy, 21st century skills, GFSL, Global Forum on School Leadership

THE IMPACT OF TECHNOLOGY AND LEARNING HISTORY

In the late 1970s and early 1980s some of those who were newly learning about the potential of the microcomputer were intent upon using it to more efficiently do what had been done in classrooms for generations (Dwyer, 1996). In classrooms around the globe, in both developing and developed countries, students were learning multiplication facts, rote learning equations, repeating the content of the next chapter in the social studies textbook, and waiting for the teacher to tell them what they were to learn next and how they were to think about the issues that were being presented to them. Subsequently, in the early years after computers had been introduced, many teachers who had learned their craft in an industrial age model were delighted that the computer freed them from the "mind-killing" (O'Brien, 1994) tedium of drill-and-practice lessons. To this stage in the evolution of computer use, it was clear that some educators had not devoted sufficient "careful thought to the kinds of teaching and learning tasks to which the microcomputer . . . [could] best be applied" (Maddux, Johnson, & Willis, 2001, p. 96).

Quite a few years later when computers facilitated access to the world's data banks, and supported text, audio, and then video conversations between learners a room apart, and then half a world away from each other, the transformational potential of these information and communications technologies (ICTs) in learning environments began to burgeon. No longer was the personal computer relegated to a world of learning typified by drill-and-practice, stand-alone programming, and teacher-directed, full class activities in a self-contained classroom space. With the new application of technology's power, what began to emerge was a new paradigm of learning that focused upon the individual learner directing, managing, and being responsible for the products of his/her own learning, with the assistance and guidance of a coach who shared in the learning experience in a teaming, partnering capacity.

THE SHIFT FROM CLASSROOM LEARNING
TO GLOBAL LEARNING ENVIRONMENTS

Decades after the advent of personal computing's patchy integration into learning environments via the faltering steps of early adopters, ICTs have been incorporated into a multitude of socio-educational activities and environments. Ubiquitous technology has provided a growing majority of the population with access to more information than has ever been readily available in human history.

The personal computer was exercising its potential for upsetting the balance of power in the classroom and in the learning process. The pendulum of power had begun to swing toward the learner who now had the tools, and the technological savvy to begin to construct his/her own meaning from experiences, explorations, and self-directed learning adventures, in collaboration with peers, with community partners, recognized experts, and with global colleagues.

Similar redistributions of power have been recognized in the global political arena, and have likewise been supported by the transformational potential of technology. De Vaney, Gance, and Yan Ma (2000) have explored the true potential of ICTs in situations where the tyranny of power has been redefined through the non-traditional use of existing technologies for the good of disenfranchised populations. They describe authentic situations where technology has created new personal potential, and increased the power available to the technology user in the global political arena.

For many readers in the western world, these case studies represent a new reality which heretofore has not forced itself into the western level of consciousness. Having chosen isolationism in previous generations of legislative policies, media coverage, and personal practices, a buffer zone has been created between western realities and the realities of the vast majority of the world's people. There existed little reason to be cognizant of the world of differing attitudes outside that buffer zone. However, the Twin Towers in New York on September 11, 2001, Bali in October 2002, Riyadh in the last months of 2003, and now Madrid in early 2004 have permanently changed the appropriateness of our practiced complacency. These events suggest that using the transformational potential of ICTs in a global learning environment is crucial to the creation of globally aware, responsible, and empowered learners capable of providing a positive direction for the evolution of the new century. Deeper applications of technology use in the classroom and on the world stage have provided increasing evidence that deep thinking, deep creativity, and deep understanding must evolve from the transformational potential of ICTs in personal and professional learning arenas.

In order for the revolution in learning capabilities to be fully incorporated into the educational system, however, it is clear that new generations of school teachers and school leaders must themselves experience alternative means of learning and thinking. This formative experience is a prerequisite if they are to develop the mental models (Senge, 2000) capable of capitalizing on the transformational potential of ICTs in 21st century learning environments.

If indeed the likelihood of the terrorist-based tragedies of the first four years of the new millennium can be ameliorated through greater understanding of alternative world views and a deeper level of honor and respect being afforded those who think and act differently than we do, then it is imperative that the Type II applications of technology discussed by Maddux, Johnson, and Willis (2001) incorporate global awareness appropriate for the technologically rich learning context of the new century.

It is in this global and technologically rich learning context that the greatest good can be realized by

1. allowing learners the active intellectual involvement required in the exploration of the realities of others from around the globe;
2. providing the learner control of the interactions that happen through the screen and the focus of discussion beyond the screen that are designed to engage learners in their own personal and professional development;
3. encouraging the learner to communicate, and to share self-constructed files, text, voice, video resources, and other inputs as a commonplace and necessary feature of deep involvement in the individual and collaborative construction of meaning on a global scale and with a global audience;

4. removing any limits to the creativity, approach, or intensity imposed on the learning processes or artifacts incorporated in exchanges; and
5. recognizing that the resultant behavior of the learner and learning partners might indeed move beyond the standard hours of the school day through the exploration of global relationships. Further, the full impact of this Type II experience might itself continue to develop and affect subsequent learning opportunities, and influence (change the direction of) personal growth and development of expertise and understanding beyond the initial experience (see Maddux et al., 2001, p. 109, for a listing of the characteristics of Type II applications upon which this global reconstruction of the typology has been based).

In the majority of Type II applications, the computer takes on the role of a tool that learners use to construct their own knowledge. However, to take school-based learning with technology beyond the realms of traditional, industrial age models of content acquisition, to student-centered engagement in authentic learning opportunities, a new vision of learning possibilities is necessary (Gibson, Schiller, Turk, & Patterson, 2003); and that vision must be shared, understood, and supported by the next generation of school leaders if it is to become reality.

THE GLOBAL FORUM ON SCHOOL LEADERSHIP

An example of Type II applications of ICTs suitable for 21st century learners can be found in the GFSL. As a Type II application of interactive computing technology, the GFSL brings together learners who share a common goal, and creates a learning partnership between them. The GFSL operates within a university graduate course context that distinguishes itself from traditional administrator preparation programs and focuses upon teamwork, collaboration, individual and collaborative construction of knowledge, the creation of professional communities of learning, integration of coursework, and heavy technology use as it applies to the re-definition of the roles of school leaders in schools designed to meet the needs of 21st century learners.

Dependent partly on the theoretical framework derived from problem-based learning (PBL) (Boud & Feletti, 1991; Bridges, 1992), this program contextualizes learning around authentic problems of practice that are explored in collaborative team settings and lead to learner-directed and setting-enhanced learning. A large portion of program activities comprises "the research-based exploration of authentic, contextualized problems of practice in collaboration with administrators, teachers, and other educational personnel from local school districts" (Gibson, 2002a, p. 2). However, "contextualizing . . . leadership experiences in traditional and unvarying cultural contexts often presents its own limitations, particularly during the formative period of leadership philosophies, perspectives, and practices" (Gibson, p. 2). Subsequently, the focus on incorporating alternative leadership contexts into class discussions through a global orientation to leadership preparation, particularly in a post September 11, 2001, international context, became a necessary focus to course development and improvement.

An investigation of the problem analysis process of PBL (De Grave, Boshuizen, & Schmidt, 1996) supports the notion that exposure to different ideas in a team setting based on collaboration and shared growth leads to conceptual change, and that "group interactions serve to encourage activation and elaboration of existing knowledge and integration of alternative views" (Gibson, 2002a, p. 2). The simple logic here, as it applies to the GFSL, is that interaction with peers and colleagues concerned with the same major professional issues, but with differing cultural slants to those issues, will produce new learning in all participants.

Since the beginning of the GFSL four semesters ago, classes of neophyte school leaders enrolled in a school leader preparation program in the United States, and similar classes of students enrolled in a school leader preparation program in Australia have participated in the GFSL. The 'global' component of the GFSL incorporates these widely separated graduate students who are studying school leadership online from many locations in Australia and Southeast Asia, interacting with students based in the Midwest of the United States, who are also studying school leadership in a predominantly face-to-face mode.

Using Blackboard as the communication medium, these learning partners dialog, share resources, collaborate, develop personal and professional relationships, share classroom activities, collaborate on course assignments, argue, reflect, research, and learn together. As they enhance their knowledge, understandings, skills, and dispositions on school leadership issues, their expertise in other, less obvious areas also expands.

These participants learn to understand differences in cultural perspectives and the subsequent impact on approaches to shared areas of interest. While most school principals are interested in similar school-related issues, these GFSL participants learn to break the nexus between culturally transmitted and traditional solutions to school leadership issues, and hear how others with different cultural and professional perspectives and experiences come to different solutions for the same problems. Learning to understand alternative conceptions and approaches to the same issues from the perspectives of their new global colleagues frees up the thinking of school leaders in training and provides them with skills that can be applied in situations where more subtle differences abound.

Further, cultural understandings impact other areas of learning associated with these interactions. While many would consider Australian and American cultures to be quite similar, it becomes obvious during these interactions that more refined understandings of each of the participating cultures are shared by both participant groups.

Other obvious learning benefits result from these interactions. While clearly dependent upon the presence and capabilities of highly interactive ICTs, the GFSL actually makes the technology invisible as the power of the global interaction takes over and the intensity of the model of learning is activated. Technophobe participants work within a strong peer network of support, and soon lose their fear of the technology.

In addition to the pure technology experience, GFSL participants also interact with quite a different model of learning. They collaborate with peers, define directions for dialog, develop responsibility for success of the learning experience, own the learning, ensure authenticity of the interactions, provide evidence that they have achieved the recognized and publicized objectives of the GFSL, collaborate with peers and global partners, act as a team, and ensure the quality of the product that is presented to the global audience of which they are part.

Having experienced for themselves another form of learning, these GFSL participants take with them to each school to which they contribute in the future, a new conception of learning that has become part of the school leader's own learning history. Consequently, the new learning model becomes an alternative in the choices available when the approach to learning is defined in that future school context. Consequently, the GFSL displays all of the hallmarks of Type II applications of technology and presents a strong argument for extending the Type II typology to include global relevance and a focus on 21st century learning skills (Partnership for 21st Century Learning, 2002) as integral constructs of the definition.

EVALUATION OF THE EFFECTIVENESS
OF THE GLOBAL FORUM ON SCHOOL LEADERSHIP

For this learning experiment, four different approaches to evaluation were adopted: A formal survey response form was expected to be completed by students at the conclusion of each GFSL; an analysis of monthly reflective logs submitted by students was undertaken; a statistical analysis of participant interaction patterns (a feature of the Blackboard course management software) was generated; and an analysis of participant postings to the discussion boards was undertaken to extract reactions related to the operation and value of the experience to participants. These data sets were able to provide a triangulated description of the operational procedures of the GFSL, and the learning benefit accruing to participants. Representative evaluation items, associated data, and a selected range of responses from all semester evaluations are organized below in sections related to forum procedure, technology learning, professional learning, cultural learning, new ways of learning, and overall reactions to the GFSL and are presented to provide a sense of the range of reactions to the GFSL experience.

Notwithstanding the four approaches taken in evaluating the GFSL, the type of questions used in various forms are represented by the following selected items: (a) Describe any previous participation in this type of online discussion, (b) What advice would you provide to make the GFSL more effective?, (c) What value has been added to your understanding of school leadership issues, online discussions as a learning tool, global perspectives to your approach to learning, and the need for increasing global sensitivity and cultural awareness?, (d) How has adding a global perspective to your learning about school leadership assisted you in your growth as a school leader?, (e) What cultural learnings were derived from your participation?, and (f) How can this online process become a viable learning tool for colleagues/students?

Forum procedure. The following comments relate to the operation of the GFSL. Advice to GFSL organizers can also be garnered from these responses: (a) It is overwhelming with all of the messages that have to be read from everyone; (b) On-line discussions are intimidating–more threatening than verbal expression in class; (c) In class, a few people dominate discussions. This does provide a level playing field; (d) I would say that there should be a certain amount of participation required each week because if you don't, then some people never make a valid contribution; and (e) I felt overwhelmed at first.

Technology learning. Some difficulties in GFSL participation could be traced directly back to user comfort with the technology. Many of the technology-related comments also fit nicely into the category related to the GFSL as a new way of learning: (a) It will help develop my leadership skills as well as develop my technological skills; (b) It is cumbersome to navigate Blackboard for the short time that I have been accessing it; and (c) Need to make it easier and make people feel more welcome to share their perspectives!

Professional learning. Comments in this category relate directly to the impact of GFSL experience on individual understanding about school leadership and associated issues: (a) I think that the forum is a very good way to discuss school leadership issues; (b) I took Blackboard training so I could use it to facilitate discussions with my teachers; and (c) A global conversation to share problems and solutions can only be good for us all!

Other data explored leadership issues, captured gems of leadership wisdom, and demonstrated the value of the professional exchange represented by the GFSL: (a) Good leadership will catch people doing things right; and (b) Being a leader means listening to others, and seeing things from all perspectives.

Cultural learning. Here, responses relate to a greater understanding of different cultures: (a) I learned we are all human beings–we share commonalities with overseas colleagues; (b) An important thing we can do is increase global sensitivity and cultural awareness; and (c) My most valuable cultural learning is that all cultures face similar successes/problems.

Responses to others' personal stories provided opportunity for greater understanding and learning about cultures and people, and the value of different perspectives they bring to an issue: (a) My family escaped from South Africa during the worst time under apartheid; (b) I am one of the boat people, first generation Vietnamese in the U.S.; and (c) I grew up in Kansas and will spend my whole life here.

New ways of learning. GFSL participants displayed a variety of comfort levels with models of learning that varied from the traditional teacher-centered model. Few had experience using technology as a tool in their own learning. These comments frame the impact of a new model of learning: (a) Love to use this for discussions with others with my same position, responsibilities; (b) The information helped me reframe some of my thoughts; (c) I have learned about a good tool to use in my own learning; (d) Forums such as this will become a main component of any class; and (e) Online discussions as a learning tool? Amazing potential!

Overall reactions to the forum. All sources of evaluative data suggested participants benefited in a variety of ways from their participation. The overall success of the GFSL was confirmed by these data: (a) I certainly encourage you to continue this type of a forum–a great learning experience; (b) I learned I am not alone. I have support and I am setting up a network of colleagues; (c) It gave insight to the similarities in educational issues beyond the continent; and (d) I think it opened my eyes–we are a global society–I should look beyond my own country.

Regardless of the style of evaluation adopted in interactive, international learning community activities such as the GFSL, it is clear that participant voices need to be heard and incorporated in future planning decisions. A variety of authentic assessment pieces is recommended, as is variety in the modes through which evaluation is mediated and collected. The ownership and responsibility for success that individual participants displayed during this experience demanded their authentic involvement in the assessment and evaluation of the innovation, and ensured improvement and growth for future GFSL versions.

The Type II Impact of the Global Forum on Participants' Learning Processes

Throughout the semester of involvement, GFSL participants increasingly display cultural and professional sensitivity to how the life experience, language, history, geography, religion, politics, culture, and context of an individual constitutes the basis of alternative perspectives. McKay (1994) explored this process from the perspective of communication theory and suggested that participants in communications, like those in the GFSL, have learned how to describe their contexts in ways that allow others to recognize the real meanings in the messages sent. The process is not unlike that to which Toffler (1995) refers as a process of "learning, unlearning, and relearning" in order to adjust to new contexts and to new participants to the communication. Further, it was one intention of this global learning project to develop the ability to send and receive messages which facilitated the emergence of self-regulated or autonomous learning (Alagic, Gibson, Doyle, Watters, & Keys, 2004), thereby providing the necessary conditions for co-construction of new knowledge and recognition of multiple perspectives in the global domain.

In addition, reflective practice was used extensively by participants to refine their thinking, and adjust their personal beliefs and attitudes (Gibson & Alagic, 2003). Co-reflective exchanges between students in large groups and in smaller more intimate dialog teams further aided the development of individual skills in recognizing and breaking down the barriers to communication. This process was central to the development of an online learning community, and it was entirely dependent upon student willingness to explore new learning contexts/procedures, develop risk-readiness, trust, and take responsibility for enterprise success. Success of these enterprises also depends upon the instructors' ability to be flexible, respond to tone/frequency of engagements, seek ongoing feedback, collaborate with others in the learning partnership, and share ownership/control of the direction of the dialog with participants (Gibson, Schiller, Turk, & Patterson, 2003).

As a result of the cognitive apprenticeship (Duncan, 1996) that GFSL participants have undergone, a variety of Type II results have accrued. Supported by the presence of interactive computer technologies, the Global Forum has been able to (a) incorporate a global orientation to leadership preparation, (b) emphasize appropriately selected technologies to achieve expanded course objectives, (c) transform the learning model traditionally employed in leader preparation programs, (d) provide evidence suggesting that there is a smarter way of thinking about technology use in learning and that it is represented not by a focus on technology but a focus on the intent of the learning activity and the way the learning environment is conceived and structured, (e) use technology to support individual growth, professional leader development, and the transformation of commonly accepted cultural stereotypes of organizational behaviors as they relate to leading in educational contexts, and (f) acknowledge the central role of school leaders in the successful integration of technology into learning environments and the transformation of traditional paradigms of learning, pedagogy, and school organization.

The deep thinking, reflection, and the construction of meaning in a global learning environment, as represented by the GFSL (Gibson, 2002b), presents an example of the currently known upper end of the evolutionary continuum of technology use in learning as described by Dwyer, Ringstaff and Sandholtz (1990). In fact, this process of instructional evolution in technology has been described, in their conception, by teachers moving from adopting technology in support of common instructional practices, to adapting technology for experimenting with different instructional practices, to appropriating technology to create new strategies, to creating learning situations where technology is used by students to invent learning experiences. At the upper end of this continuum, teachers who choose to incorporate ubiquitous ICTs into their learning environments have generated a context where learning opportunities themselves are ubiquitous and, conceivably, extend to a global scale. Selby and Pike (2000) do not see this as a choice, however, suggesting that "worldmindedness," as they call it, is no longer a luxury, but a necessity for survival in the new century. They suggest that encountering diverse viewpoints and perspectives engenders a richer understanding of self, concluding that personal discovery is critical to self-fulfillment and to the generation of constructive change on a global scale. Pike (2000) corroborates through an emphasis upon the interdependence of all people within a global system. He recognizes that within a school learning context, this is more often than not expressed in terms of the connections between students in one country with people and environments in other parts of the world and the resulting insights, ideas, and information that enable students to look beyond the confines of local and national boundaries in their thinking and aspirations.

Students in our schools today live in an increasingly complex and interrelated world (Calder, 2000). To be effective in dealing with this new type of learner in their schools, educational leaders must actively recognize that their worlds are changing too and develop a vision for education where technology applications support deep learning processes (Taylor, 1998), and where they realize that Type II applications of technologies emphasize the learning process and the theory and philosophy behind it, and "are only part of the instructional approach that determines their success" (Maddux et al., 2001, p. 109).

Expectations for education are changing. The knowledge base of education is changing. Conceptions of how individual learning occurs are changing. The tools available to "do" education are changing. The roles of teachers are changing. Understandings of what should be learned, who should be learning, how they should learn, where they should learn, and when they should learn are changing. So, expecting school leaders to recreate their conceptions of what constitutes appropriate leader behavior should also change! Technology applications, like the GFSL, make available "new and better ways of teaching and learning" (Maddux et al., 2001, p. 101) and represent one way of extending the Type II potential of information and communication technology to new school leaders who are learning their trade in the technology-rich, global learning arena of the 21st century.

REFERENCES

Alagic, M., Gibson, K. L., Doyle, C., Watters, J., & Keys, P. (2004). The potential for autonomous learning through ICT. *Proceedings of the 15th International Conference of the Society for Information Technology & Teacher Education* (pp. 1679-1684). Atlanta, GA.

Boud, D., & Feletti, G. (Eds.). (1991). *The challenge of problem based learning.* London: Kogan Page.

Bridges, E. M. (1992). *Problem based learning for administrators.* ERIC Clearinghouse on Educational Management.

Calder, M. (2000). A concern for justice: Teaching using a global perspective in the classroom. *Theory into Practice, 39*(2), 81-87.

De Grave, W., Boshuizen, H., & Schmidt, H. (1996). Problem based learning: Cognitive and metacognitive processes during problem analysis. *Instructional Science,* (24), 321-341.

De Vaney, A., Gance, S., & Ma, Y. (Eds.). (2000). *Technology and resistance: Digital communications and new coalitions around the world.* New York: Peter Lang.

Duncan, S. (1996). Cognitive apprenticeship in classroom instruction: Implications for industrial and technical education. *Journal of Industrial Teacher Education, 33*(3), 66-86.

Dwyer, D. (1996). The imperative to change our schools. In C. Fisher, D. Dwyer, & K. Yocam (Eds.), *Education and technology: Reflections on computing in classrooms* (pp. 15-33). San Francisco, CA: Jossey-Bass.

Dwyer, D., Ringstaff, C., & Sandholtz, J. (1990). *The evolution of teachers' instructional beliefs and practices in high-access-to-technology classrooms.* Paper presented at the meeting of the American Education Research Association, Boston, MA.

Gibson, I. W. (2002a). Masters in Educational Administration–The Global Forum on School Leadership. Global Learning Development Grant Application. Wichita State University.

Gibson, I. W. (2002b). Developing a Global Forum on School Leadership: Using interactive communications technology to enhance the achievement of learning goals in a school leader preparation program. *Proceedings of the World Conference on Educational Multimedia, Hypermedia & Telecommunications* (pp. 612-613). Denver, CO.

Gibson, I. W., Schiller, J., Turk, R., & Patterson, J. (2003). International, on-line learning communities: Expanding the learning and technology horizons of new school leaders. *Proceedings of the 14th International Conference of the Society for Information Technology & Teacher Education,* Albuquerque, NM.

Gibson, K. L., & Alagic, M. (2003). Teacher's reflective practice: Adding a global learning facet. *Proceedings of the Conference for Innovation in Higher Education,* Kiev, Ukraine.

Maddux, C. D., Johnson, D. L., & Willis, J. W. (2001). *Educational computing: Learning with tomorrow's technologies* (3rd ed.). Needham Heights, MA: Allyn & Bacon.

McKay, H. (1994). *Why don't people listen? Solving the communication problem.* Sydney: Pan.

O'Brien, T. C. (1994). Computers in education: A Piagetian perspective. In I. J. J. Hirschbuhl (Ed.), *Computers in education* (pp. 12-14). Guildford, CT: Dushkin.

Partnership for 21st Century Skills. (2002). *Learning for the 21st century.* Washington, DC: Author.

Pike, G. (2000). Global education and national identity: In pursuit of meaning. *Theory into Practice, 39*(2), 64-73.

Selby, D., & Pike, G. (2000). Civil global education: Relevant learning for the twenty-first century. *Convergence, 33*(1/2), 138-149.

Senge, P. M. (2000). *Schools that learn: A fifth discipline fieldbook for educators, parents, and everyone who cares about education.* New York: Doubleday.

Taylor, H. (1998). How in the world does one teach global education? *Momentum, 29*(3), 16-18

Toffler, A., &. Toffler, H. (1995). *Creating a new civilization.* Atlanta, GA: Turner.

Index

© 2005 by The Haworth Press, Inc. All rights reserved.

T - #0548 - 101024 - C0 - 212/152/11 - PB - 9780789024954 - Gloss Lamination